Education & Training on the Internet

An essential resource for students, teachers and education providers

Internet Handbooks

Other titles in preparation

Education &
Training
on the internet

An essential resource for students, teachers
and education providers

Laurel Alexander
MIPD MICG

www.internet-handbooks.co.uk

Other Internet Handbooks by the same author

Careers Guidance on the Internet
Graduate Job Hunting on the Internet
Overseas Job Hunting on the Internet
Human Resource Management on the Internet
Working from Home on the Internet

First published in 2000 by Internet Handbooks, a Division of International
Briefings Ltd, Plymbridge House, Estover Road, Plymouth PL6 7PY,
United Kingdom.

Customer services tel:	(01752) 202301
Orders fax:	(01752) 202333
Customer services email:	cservs@plymbridge.com
Distributors web site:	http://www.plymbridge.com
Internet Handbooks web site:	http://www.internet-handbooks.co.uk

Note: The contents of this book are offered for the purposes of general
guidance only and no liability can be accepted for any loss or expense incurred
as a result of relying in particular circumstances on statements made in this
book. Readers are advised to check the current position with the appropriate
authorities before entering into personal arrangements.

Case studies in this book are entirely fictional and any resemblance to real
persons or organisations is entirely coincidental.

Printed and bound by The Cromwell Press Ltd, Trowbridge, Wiltshire.

Contents

Contents . . . .

List of illustrations

Illustrations . . . .

Preface

This book has been written by an educator for educators. I produced it partly as a professional project, and partly because I love learning, and have learned a great deal myself through researching it.

Whether you are looking for web sites to help you, or whether you are thinking of creating your own education and training web site, the internet offers unparalleled opportunities for learning and self-development. We can also learn about the new technology itself, and how to apply it in education and training. It is wonderful to see how people everywhere are embracing the net to develop and deliver learning opportunities for people hungry to acquire new knowledge and skills. So many education and training opportunities are available at the press of a key or click of a mouse – what are you waiting for?

The internet is an enormous boon for the concept of lifelong learning, and can support it at every level:

▶ *Individual learning* – In a rapidly-changing world, we all need to improve and update our skills and knowledge throughout our lives, whatever our original background. Forget the experiences of school days. Learning is something we do every day. In taking responsibility for our own learning, we can create new opportunities for ourselves, new self-perceptions, relationships, and life choices.

▶ *Family learning* – Children, parents, and other family members are involved together in learning activities. Children are often more knowledgeable and skilled in the internet than adults, so adults and children can learn from each other about computers and the best way to use them. Most homes now have a PC, and thousands more people are going online. When we develop as individuals, both the family and the individuals gain.

▶ *Community learning* – Can take endless forms, from a catering or language class at a local leisure centre, to a return to work and study project run by a university and a Social Service Family Centre on a housing estate. Part at least may take place on educational premises; for example, classes in computing and internet skills. It produces benefits for both individuals and the wider community.

▶ *Business learning* – As operating companies become leaner and more diverse in delivery, networking becomes essential. To survive and prosper, we need to network effectively with colleagues, suppliers, advisers, community representatives, customers and clients. The internet itself is the greatest network of all, and the minute we go online we are networking electronically – developing ecommerce, using online courses, or browsing for resources to help us. We can link to others nationally and internationally for professional development and for business opportunities.

Preface

The internet crosses all traditional boundaries geographical, national, cultural, institutional, economic, political, and linguistic. It enables us to see our own situation in a wider context, to make connections between local and global events, and to attract wider interest in our projects. It allows us to identify common interests and to develop solidarity with individuals and communities almost anywhere.

Internet technology offers a new challenge, not only to education and training, but to the whole way human beings live and work. It represents as big a challenge as any great revolution of the past. It is comparable perhaps with the invention of the printed word in the fifteenth century, the new technology of the day. Spreading information cheaply, quickly and in many languages other than Latin, the printed word shook the old medieval authorities to their foundations, and marked a new renaissance in culture, beliefs, science and exploration.

This new world of instant and borderless communications can seem scary, and with very good reason. Unable or unwilling to adapt, many of the traditional institutions we take for granted will not survive, unable to attract funding, or the right customer or public support for the future. As individual professionals we must rapidly learn to adapt our own thinking and skills to meet the challenge of the internet revolution.

As you traverse the web of learning and come across worthwhile sites for education and training, please email your discoveries to me that I may include them in future books, and as links on my web site.

Laurel Alexander

http://www.flexiblelearning.co.uk
laurelalexander@internet-handbooks.co.uk

1 Learning and technology

In this chapter we will explore:

▶ *the rise of open and distance learning*
▶ *new learning technologies*
▶ *internet basics*
▶ *why use the web for learning?*
▶ *online learning*
▶ *virtual universities*
▶ *education and training on the internet*

. . . .

We have always had the opportunity of learning through technology –
after all, pens were a technological innovation! There is the technology of
TV such as the *Learning Zone* on BBC2 which provides programmes for
groups with specific educational needs such as OU students, key professional groups, FE students, managers and employees of SMEs. Learning
technology resources such as OHPs, slide projectors, laser pointers and
self-cleaning whiteboards are fast becoming dinosaurs of the learning
technology game. New learning technologies today means virtual
universities, online learning, computer-aided learning and computer-
mediated communications.

The rise of open and distance learning

Distance and open learning are ways of delivering a flexible learning
programme which learners can adapt to suit their individual working
circumstances (financial or time). Soren Nipper (1989) suggested the
concept of three generations of distance education. The single medium,
correspondence-type model represented the first generation. UK Open
University was the earliest major model of second generation distance
education which used one-way media print, broadcasting and cassettes
backed up by two-way communication (tutors). The third generation is
built upon the use of electronic information systems such as audio tele-
conferencing, computer conferencing and video conferencing.

New learning technologies

These refer to ways in which we can use technology and computers for
learning.

Computer Aided Assessment (CAA)
CAA is the new buzz-word taking over from CAL (Computer Aided
Learning). It can be used to support open and computer based interactive flexible learning opportunities and involves processing learners'
answers by computer.

Learning and technology...

Computer Aided Learning (CAL)

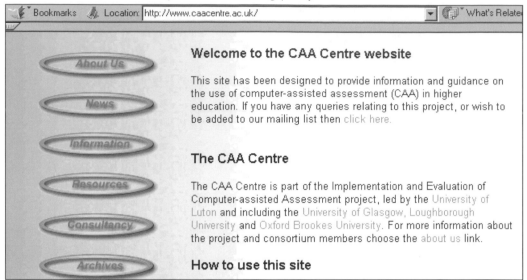

Fig. 1. The Computer Assisted Assessment Centre being developed by a consortium of UK universities.

This refers to multimedia or computer-aided instruction. The term multimedia was originally used by institutions running distance learning courses in which they delivered content via a combination of text, TV, telephone, audio cassette and the radio. The new twist to the tale is the way in which we now use computers to bring these things together. High-resolution screens and sound and video playback in computers have resulted in the increased use of multimedia applications for learning.

A multimedia program is designed to support the learning process and offers the experience of listening, looking and doing in a computer-mediated setting. It can be interesting and motivating and help students achieve understanding in new ways. The use of sound, photographs and video enables the user to observe real-world situations, which is not possible with the more conventional methods of instruction. There is also a high level of interaction. Most packages expect learners to make choices about what they want to do next and how they wish to work through the material. Therefore there is a degree of empowerment to the learner. Six main elements make up a typical multimedia program: text, sound, images, animation, movies, and user control. An example of a multimedia user is the OU's Knowledge Media Institute. This has developed 'the virtual microscope', a multimedia emulation of a science experiment. It has been particularly successful with learners with physical and visual impairments unable to use conventional microscopes.

Computer-Based Learning (CBL)
This can apply to either computer-aided instruction (CAI) which is used mainly in education or computer-based training (CBT) or job-orientated training.

Computer-Mediated Communications (CMC)
Online conferencing or discussion forums mimic real face-to-face discus-

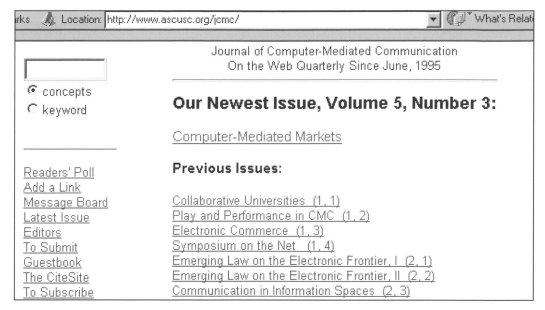

Journal of Computer-Mediated Communication
On the Web Quarterly Since June, 1995

sions. They make it easy to share information and create a 'knowledge base' that people can access at any time. They can also reduce the need for meetings and save time by exchanging ideas and information through discussion groups. Discussion groups are more sophisticated than email, as they can provide structured forums for discussions and link related topics. Many also allow you to view the information in a variety of ways: by person, by topic, by date. Online conferencing can be used in a variety of ways:

1. virtual seminars which can be facilitator-moderated and directed
2. online support with tutor/trainer and peer support on a range of issues relevant to the course
3. national and international conferencing with timed events to discuss topical issues or support a conference
4. distance team work with virtual meetings, discussions and papers on-line
5. distance peer discussion.

Digital Technology
The term digital is a reference to something based on binary digits or numbers or their representation.

1. Digital video-interactive is a hardware/software system developed by RCA, General Electric and Intel that implement compression of digital video and audio for microcomputer applications.

2. Digital simultaneous voice and data technology has been patented by Multi-Tech Systems and allows a single telephone line to be used for conversation together with data transfer.

3. Digital Video Disc (DVD) is the next generation of optical disc storage

Fig. 2. The *Journal of Computer-Mediated Communication* is a handy way of keeping up to date in this field. It reports on processes in communication networks, privacy, economic and access issues.

technology. Using this technology video, audio and computer data can be encoded onto a compact disc. These discs can store larger amounts of data than a traditional CD. As Josh Hillman, Head of Education Policy at the BBC, says: 'Digital broadcasting, the internet and multimedia software now add a whole new range of possibilities for interactive and customised learning. More and more people are using online services as sources of information and learning and the BBC's online learning service is the most heavily used education web site in Europe.'

Groupware
A term used to describe software to enable a group of users on a network to collaborate on a particular project.

Information and Communications Technology (ICT)
Using this approach, learners keep in touch with the tutor and each other via email. Support feedback in the school or workplace is essential and it is useful to encourage learners to coach each other and work together to improve performance. There is a large degree of autonomy in this method of learning and individuals need to take responsibility for their own development.

Interactive Compact Disc (CD-I)
This is a hardware and software standard that can combine audio, video and text on high-capacity compact discs.

Fig. 3. The UK National Grid For Learning (NGfL). This government-backed site is a good example of how school and college learning communities can be connected together using the world wide web.

Virtual Learning Communities
Henley Management College has been working with IBM using Lotus Learning Space, an advanced groupware product. Its objective has been to create extended virtual communities to provide a platform for people on an MBA programme. Learners attend workshops but also work

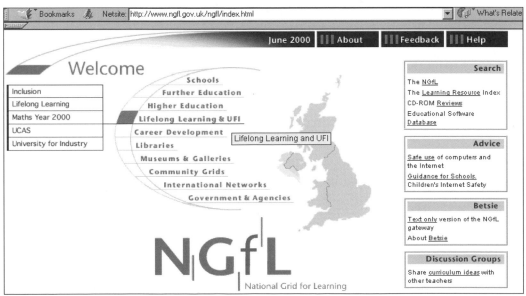

through the programme in the intervening periods within Learning Space. They are organised into study groups that interact virtually, with the support of a tutor. Electronic connections exist within study groups, between study groups and between the study groups and the tutor. Extended learning communities provide access to online experts and to a shared knowledge and resource base.

Virtual World Learning
A 3-D modelled environment where a user can interact with the viewer. This could be through a simulator.

Internet basics

What is the internet?
The internet, which originated in America in the late sixties, is a vast international network of computers linked up to exchange information. At the core of the internet are powerful computers that are permanently connected to each other. Other computers or PCs can dial into these larger systems via a modem and telephone line.

How can you access the internet?
In order to get onto the internet or to have your own web site, you need a computer, a modem (which links your computer to a telephone line), and an account with an internet access provider. The minimum hardware you would need would be an IBM-compatible 486 computer or a Macintosh 68030 series with a minimum of 8 megabytes of RAM.

What can you do with the internet?
You can 'surf the web' and visit web sites across the globe. There are literally millions of web sites covering any subject you can think of. Some sites reflect personal interests, e.g. someone into connoisseur wines might have their own site telling visitors about different wines they've tasted across the globe. Other sites are more informative, e.g. cancer support or showing how disabled people can work from home. Then there are the commercial sites where a product or a service is being sold, e.g. book publishers or career guidance organisations.

Ecommerce is a huge and rapidly growing part of the internet, and refers to conducting business over the internet. We can now do our banking through the internet, take an online degree, do our supermarket shopping, take an MBA in management through the internet, order clothes and books. You can even go online to a virtual therapist and have a stress management consultation. If you can imagine it, it probably exists on the internet.

You could have your own web site on the internet. You access web site space through an internet service provider (see below). You can advertise your company, sell goods or services or if you're a training provider, you can provide online courses to learners.

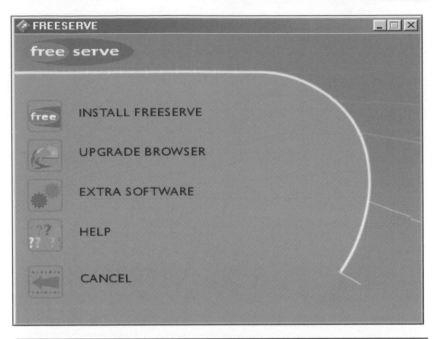

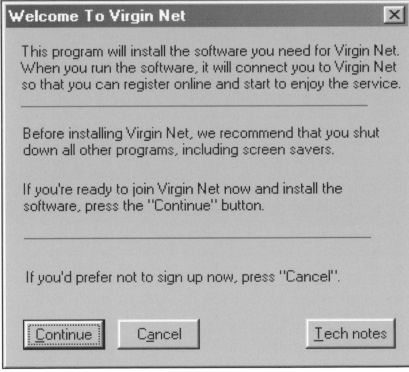

Fig. 4. Four UK internet service providers (ISPs), Freeserve, Virgin Net, Madasafish, and America Online (AOL). Their services differ in some respects, but the main purpose of each is to connect you to the internet.

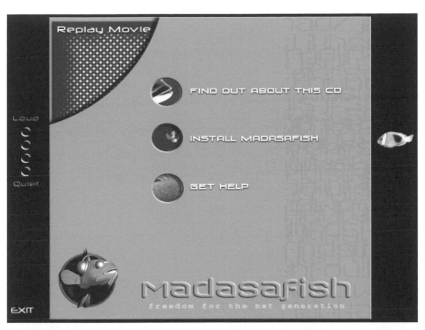

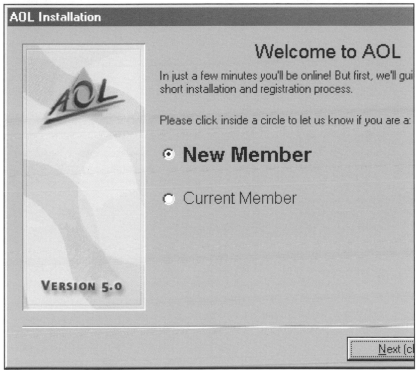

Internet access provider (IAP)
'Access' means the capability of a user to connect to the internet. The usual way is through an internet access provider (IAP) via a modem connected to the user's computer (used by majority of home computer users). The second way is through a dedicated line that is connected to a local area network (used by larger companies and organisations).

Internet service provider (ISP)
An internet service provider gives users a range of services (e.g. email accounts, newsgroups, chat rooms, free web space) in addition to simple internet access.

Browsers
This term refers to the software that lets a user view documents on the web. Using a browser you can download files (copy data from the internet). By far the two most popular browsers are Netscape Navigator and Microsoft Internet Explorer, but there are others such as Opera and NetCaptor.

Search engines
These enable you to search for a particular subject on the web. There are many excellent search engines and directories such as AltaVista, Excite, Infoseek, Lycos, UK Directory and Yahoo!.

Intranet
This is a private network designed along internet principles, but designed for information management and information flow within a company or organisation. It can also include services such as access to databases, software distribution, document distribution, and training.

Extranet
This is an extension of an intranet. It uses web technology to facilitate communication with external parties, e.g. customers, or other learning institutes, in order to enhance the speed and efficiency of their relationship.

Why use the web for learning?

The web represents a new way of looking at learning – at how it is organised and how it is presented. The web is delivery medium, content provider, and subject matter all in one. Information on the web is organised in an ever-expanding network of nodes and links that represent the more traditional domains of knowledge. Using the web, tutors and designers can create maps to guide their learners through a new world. Creating these maps, called web pages, is a relatively simple task, using powerful tools and a kind of word-processing language called hypertext markup language (HTML).

When to use the web
The web uses text and graphics interactively, and to a lesser extent video and audio. According to Reiser and Gagne's media selection diagram

---

Inside Yahoo!

- Yahoo! Address Book: Keep your contacts safe
- Web Access For Free! With Yahoo! Online
- New to Yahoo!? - For help click here

[more features...]

(Reiser and Gagne, 1983) and Merrill and Goodman's strategy and media selection technique (Merrill and Goodman, 1972) these characteristics make the web most useful when used to explore intellectual and verbal knowledge, and to a lesser extent when exploring affective learning. With its versatility and interconnectedness the web offers one of the most effective ways to work with learners who are widespread geographically. Plus the fact that the ease of use of HTML makes web based instruction (WBI) easy to update to meet the needs of changing subject matter.

When not to use the web

The web is not an option if your learners have no access to an internet-connected computer. Given that text is the primary mode of communication on the web, it is necessary that your learners are literate, or at least be approaching literacy. The web should also not be used if your instruction requires a great deal of audio or video, such as teaching psychomotor and other mostly physical procedural skills. On the other hand, if these skills can be successfully taught using primarily still graphics, it is possible to use the web.

Advantages and disadvantages of using the web

Through helper applications and internal mechanisms the web can connect a learner to almost any part of the internet. Because of this, the web shares the advantages and disadvantages of the rest of the internet. McManus' description of the internet fits the web well:

'The internet can deliver video, but not as quickly as videotape, television, or CD-rom. It can carry real-time personal interaction, but not as well as telephone or video conferencing. It can display textual information, but not a usefully as a book or magazine. Why then should the Internet ever be used? The net has two real advantages over other media. It combines advantages of other media so that it conveys video and sound better than a book, is more interactive than a videotape and, unlike a CD-rom, it can link people from around the world cheaply. The second advantage, and one that is often overlooked when discussing the Internet as a delivery system, is that it can also be a content provider. The internet is, arguably, the largest and most diverse information resource in the world today. It is possible to incorporate the wealth of information available on the net in your design. For instance if you are designing a module on renaissance art history, you can include links to the Vatican Library and the Louvre, as well as to the Art History exhibit of the Australian National University, just to name a few. This sort of immediate access to information and resources can not be found with any other medium.' (McManus, 1995).

Online learning

You can take a course 'delivered' to you over the internet. All you need is a PC with internet access and a browser such as Internet Explorer or Netscape Navigator. Typical online learning might contain a specific amount of hours of downloadable self-study modules, a specific amount of hours for dedicated tutorial support, discussion groups,

Learning and technology...

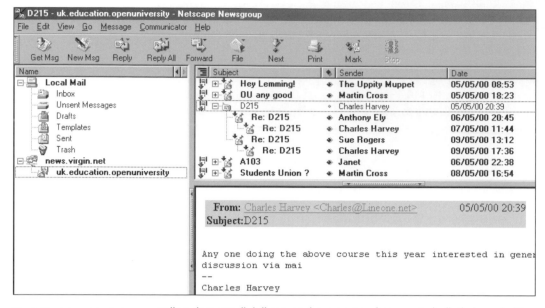

Fig. 5. The internet includes some 80,000 newsgroups (collectively called Usenet). People use them to read and post millions of messages and files covering every imaginable topic. This picture illustrates a lively newsgroup called 'uk.education.openuniversity'.

online chat, email delivery and support and access to bulletin boards. You could use professional online training providers. Or if you have an active intranet, you could be part of an internal online learning programme.

Discussion groups
This term refers to an online forum in which people communicate about subjects of common interest. Internet newsgroups ('Usenet') and electronic mailing lists are the most common forums.

Chat
Chat is a form of synchronous communication - synchronous (meaning simultaneously) as opposed to asynchronous (taking place at different times). This tool can provide learner-instructor interaction or learner-learner interaction. The best known versions are IRC (internet relay chat) and ICQ ('I seek you').

Email
Email provides one-to-one online asynchronous (messages are posted, read and replied to over a period of time, rather than in real time) communication. It can be used in a variety of ways in teaching and learning, for example:

1. disseminating information
2. linking special groups of learners
3. linking tutors/trainers and learners
4. emailing assignments
5. email tutorials for learners
6. to give learners information, updates, feedback, announcements
7. for quick responses such as setting up of meetings.

Email can be used on a course in a number of ways. Traditionally it has been used in a learner-tutor context. Learners often submit projects by way of email attachments (attached files of text or illustrations). Learners find it more useful as a conduit for information retrieval from the tutor. These are often the 'How do I...?' or 'What is required for...?' questions that tutors often get.

Email has greatly increased the interaction of between tutors and learners. Before email, learners had to ask a question in class or ask a question of the tutor before or after class. Now the tutor is available 24 hours a day, 7 days a week – which could be seen as an increase in workload. But before the advent of email those questions may never have been asked or answered. It is a great advance as far as learning is concerned.

Email also can be used to promote discussion. This would be a use of learner-to-learner interaction. Depending upon subject matter, group discussions can facilitate learning. In addition, course 'listservs' can be set up as a way to broadcast information to the group.

Bulletin Board System (BBS) (or Conferencing Tool)
BBS refers to a computer system equipped with one or more modems or other means of network access that serves as an information and message-passing centre for remote users. Learners dial into a BBS with their modems and post messages to other BBS learners. It is very like posting messages on a corkboard. Some BBS allow users to chat online and download and upload files. They can provide comments, questions and answers from the learners as well as messages from trainers. These functions make bulletin boards an important tool for teaching and learning. Using BBS, you can find information about courses, communicate with other participants on courses, ask questions and give support to fellow learners. You can:

1. post messages

2. read messages

3. search for messages

The bulletin board system is really a central communications tool for most web course development packages. This tool is an electronic version of the familiar bulletin board in the hallways of most places of learning. Learners and tutors all have access and can record information for all to see. This is a form of asynchronous communication that allows for all three forms of interaction (learner-tutor, learner-learner, and learner-content).

Virtual universities

You can study online, at university level with institutes across the world. Accredited public and private California universities offer more than 2,000 online courses to students anywhere on the web. The Open University (OU) has online resources, a site for former OU students and OU library web site. It provides links to electronic journals, texts and newspapers, library catalogues, bibliographic databases, statistical resources, and software archives. Additional services include links to and information about online resources in business and management, including company information and reports, electronic journals, newspapers, conference proceedings, library catalogues and government information resources. Another online service helps users make decisions on what to study and offers a variety of online workshops.

Education and training on the internet

The nine sections that follow this chapter are categorised as follows:

1. schools and college web sites
2. university web sites
3. vocational training web sites
4. occupational training web sites
5. adult education web sites
6. distance and online learning web sites
7. specialist web sites for particular groups
8. best of the rest web sites
9. your own education and training web site

Fig. 6(a). Here is a window from one of the pages from the hugely popular Amazon web site. Using its catalogue of a million-plus items, you can easily order almost any book, CD and video dealing with education, training and distance learning.

Some of the sites are for information only; some are encouraging you to contact them for further information while others are selling packs and courses.

Textbooks can be purchased or even downloaded over the internet: download from: http://www.cs.cmu.edu/web/books.html; to purchase go to : http://www.amazon.com and http://www.blackwell.com

You can apply for courses through many of the sites. Some institutes have on-screen forms that you can complete and then directly submit. Other ways to apply are via email or a print-off application form. You can also pay for courses over the internet with credit card or cheque.

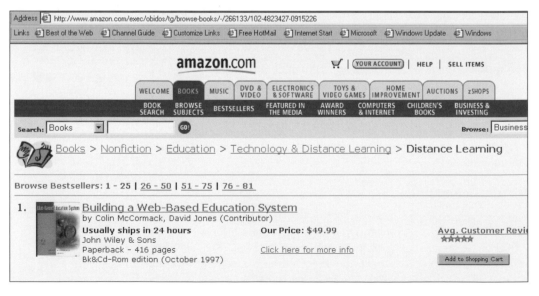

▶ *Note* – Make sure you are in a secure payment area. You will not be in a secure area unless your browser displays a message to the effect that 'You are about to enter a secure area').

As with any educational institute or organisation offering learning opportunities, check what you are getting for your money and the validity of any qualification.

The web sites reviewed were live at the time of writing.

Visit the free Internet HelpZone at
www.internet-handbooks.co.uk
Helping you master the internet

Fig. 6(b). The home page of Blackwells, one of the best-known academic online booksellers.

2 Schools & colleges

In this chapter we will explore:

▶ *schools on the internet*
▶ *further education*
▶ *learning resources*
▶ *teachers and parents*
▶ *educational technology*

Technology is now firmly entrenched into education – not only as a subject in itself but also as part of the learning process. Through the use of computers and CD-ROMs, education has widened its potential and learning has become multi-dimensional. Learners can now access subject information and they can develop technological skills. Perhaps more importantly than this, the internet allows learners to globally interact and learn from each other. Many schools have an internet presence that in itself is educational. But it is when schools link with each other across a country and beyond that a new facet of learning takes place. We discover new ways of learning and how to chat across cultures. Schools and colleges can link via virtual classrooms and develop international collaboration on common issues.

There are masses of resources for teachers and lecturers in terms of support, news and information as well as teaching resources. It might be seen as part of a teacher or tutor's development to exchange resources and learning plans with other professionals.

The internet comes into its own when it comes to home study. Homework becomes more fun if you can surf on the side. Also, students who are unable to get to school or college can still access learning opportunities or even take part in an online course.

There are five sections in this chapter:

1. Schools – online schools, revision resources, virtual reality classrooms, linking projects, consultancy services and international collaboration.

2. Further education – resources for students and lecturers, online activities, funding, news and FE job vacancies.

3. Learning resources – linking opportunities, independent learning resources, curriculum resources, home education, groupware, online learning, lesson plans, competitions, articles and information.

4. Teachers and parents – statistics, curriculum information, school profiles and inspections, teacher training, professional development, discussions groups and teacher chat.

5. Educational technology – electronic mentoring, web site design, videoconferencing and computer education.

Schools on the internet

American School Directory (USA)
http://www.asd.com/
This is a substantial gateway to all 108,000 high schools in the United States. You can use it to link to the web sites for each school. The web site includes detailed K-12 school information, free student email, a guest book, message board, calendar, wish list, alumni registration, local weather, pictures, and many other features.

AT&T Virtual Classroom (Asia/Pacific)
http://www.att.virtualclassroom.org/
The AT&T Virtual Classroom is a free online educational program for elementary, junior and senior high schools around the world. This site is designed to give primary and secondary students an opportunity to learn how to collaborate in an international setting. It runs the Clubhouse, a year-round program in which schools from all over the world can meet and work together. A matching database is used to register your own school and to search for other schools that want to work with you. The Virtual Classroom provides various online facilities and servers to help them collaborate.

Fig. 7. The Virtual Classroom developed by AT&T offers all kinds of free activities and resources through its web site. Use its search function to find the information you want.

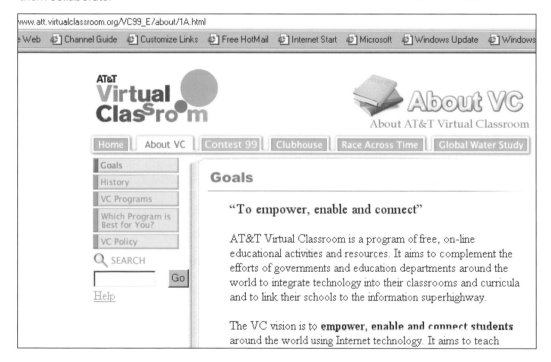

BBC Education: Schools Online (UK)
http://www.bbc.co.uk/education/schools/
This substantial and attractively presented site offers resources for all ages, including revision materials, interactive links, plus educational and general news. It includes Bitesize revision: 'Solve your study problems, and either Ask a Teacher, or let off steam with a good Screech.'

British Council Interlink Project (UK and NZ)
http://www.interlink.org.nz/
This was an online communication initiative linking British and New Zealand schools from March to July 1997. During that time more than 1,000 students from 12 schools in New Zealand and 12 in Britain communicated with each other and worked on projects together across the web. This site is a record of their achievements and a model for other schools and students who want to explore cyberspace and use it to get to know people around the world. Many of the paired schools have maintained the links they made during the project and are continuing to work together. The project welcomes contacts from other schools.

California Virtual High School Project (USA)
http://www.vhs.ucsc.edu
The California Virtual High School developed a virtual reality classroom where students could meet inside a classroom around a table. Synchronous discussions with real-time review of materials and web sites were enabled. This (archive) site illustrates a virtual tour, and links.

Canada's School Net (Canada)
http://www.schoolnet.ca
School Net is a co-operative initiative of Canada's provincial, territorial and federal governments, educators, universities and colleges and industry. It aims to link all of Canada's 16,000 plus schools to the electronic highway. Designed in an attractive magazine format, it presents a set of internet-based educational resources for teachers and learners. The site can be viewed in English and French.

CoVis: Learning Through Collaborative Visualisation (USA)
http://www.covis.nwu.edu/
CoVis was a community of thousands of students, teachers, and researchers working together to find new ways of developing science teaching and learning. The project was completed in 1998. This research is being continued under the auspices of the Center for Learning Technologies in Urban Schools and a number of other research projects in the Learning Sciences Program at Northwestern University.

Educators (UK)
http://www.educators.co.uk
This service provides tutors and trainers for various exam subjects and levels. There are links to online discussion forums, the educators' shops, games and quizzes, GCSE links and other links for educators.

EduWeb (UK)
http://www.eduweb.co.uk/
EduWeb is a well-known and substantial UK internet education service intended for use by teachers and pupils. It is full of resources for schools to communicate with other schools, to help them publish their own web pages, and to find all kinds of education links.

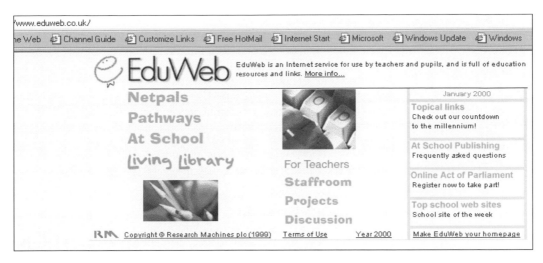

European Council of International Schools (Europe)

http://www.ecis.org/

Founded in 1965, ECIS is a membership organisation of some 500 international primary and secondary schools, from Japan in the east to the United States in the west, and from Norway in the north to Australia in the south. The site includes several searchable online directories.

European Independent Schools (Europe)

http://www.cobisec.org/

The Council of British Independent Schools in the European Communities (COBISEC) provides a directory of schools throughout Europe. The organisation was founded in 1981. It now has 33 members in 12 European countries representing about 10,000 students.

Gabbitas Educational Consultants (UK)

http://www.gabbitas.co.uk

This site offers independent guidance for parents, student and UK schools. From the home page you can order Gabbitas books (schools for special needs and independent schools). There are links for parents and students into educational advisory and guardianship services. Schools can link into appointments and consultancy services while teachers can find teaching opportunities in the UK and abroad. Gabbitas produces its own newsletter that can be accessed online. There is a contact section and special feature page.

Global Schoolhouse (USA)

http://www.gsh.org/

The home page of this site 'links kids, teachers and parents around the world'. The 'site at a glance' icon links you to a site map, search facility and contact points. Another icon on the home page leads you lessons and projects such as the cyberschoolbus and an ocean challenge. The Teacher and Parent icon links to a large range of resources. Other links on the home page include kids and teens, membership (for educators), partners and sponsors, and a bookstore.

Fig. 8. Eduweb is an established online service for UK schools, teachers and students. It has been developed by the Oxfordshire-based educational computer company Research Machines Ltd (RML).

Schools & colleges ....

Good Schools Guide (UK)
http://www.goodschoolsguide.co.uk/
This is an independent and critical published guide to British schools, written by and for parents. It includes school descriptions, as well as advice on how to choose and be accepted. If you buy the book, you will get one year's free access to the web site. The site also includes a useful resource area for parents, teachers and students.

Hobson's Guide to UK Boarding Schools (UK)
http://www.boardingschools.hobsons.com/
From this site you can link into advice, profiles and a prospectus service.

Independent Schools Directory (UK)
http://www.indschools.co.uk
This is a searchable multimedia database of about 2,000 independent schools in the UK. You can use it to find a particular school or to search for schools geographically and by various other criteria.

Independent Schools Information Service (UK)
http://www.isis.org.uk/
The site contains a comprehensive and authoritative guide to independent schools in the UK with full details on more than 1,300 schools. The site includes a search feature. A useful site map includes direct links to all pages and downloadable files on the site.

Learn OnLine (USA)
http://www.learnonline.com/
This is an independent commercial educational service that brings the classroom into your home. It serves families with children from pre-school to high school ages. 'Your children can learn about fine art by linking their computer to the Louvre museum in Paris. Or they can take a science course by using full-color images from a NASA deep space probe. And they can even take an online foreign language course from instructors that actually live and teach in their native countries. It's all out there on the Internet and the world wide web, and our online courseware brings it directly into your home!'

Northern Ireland WWW Schools Registry (UK)
http://www.stran-ni.ac.uk/pages/ni-schools.html
This is a comprehensive directory of school and educational web pages, together with information about the local education system. The web site is maintained at Stranmillis University College, Belfast. It also covers further and higher education and contains some useful educational links.

Positive Trends in Learning (USA)
http://www.newhorizons.org/positivetrends.html
Positive Trends in Learning is a published report relating to education in schools, commissioned by IBM in 1991. Although some of the examples may have changed, the trends discussed are still current. The authors would like to add new examples from parents, schools, higher education, adult education, and corporate training programs.

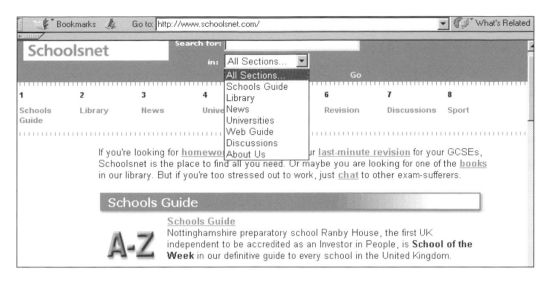

Schools Net (UK)

http://www.schoolsnet.com/

Here you can obtain a definitive illustrated guide to just about every school in the UK, including its examination results, inspection reports, background details, and other information. Click on the regional map to find schools in a particular area. Or you can try its advanced search to identify schools by age group, type of school, region and sex of pupils.

Study Web (USA)

http://www.studyweb.com/

This is a useful educational gateway site. You can follow all kinds of links from the home page with its subject classifications, or use the search function, to access more than 120,000 web pages. There is a teacher net and parent education web rings. Clicking onto the 'resource directory' will take you into educational products and services for students, teachers, parents and school administrators. There are icons linking to a software store, the classroom internet, and homework help online. Studyweb is part of Lightspan.

Tutor 2U Economics (UK)

http://www.tutor2u.com/

'A tutor at your fingertips'. A-level economists will find this a useful site. You can access case studies, economic news analysis, a glossary, essay plans, quizzes and discussions, and tackle an economics crossword.

UK Schools Internet Directory (UK)

http://www.liv.ac.uk/ ~ evansjon/directory/index.html

This site lists many UK primary and secondary schools and colleges using the internet. You can access online schools through this site, and get your own school listed. The page is part of a web site called UK School Resources, an attempt to create a 'springboard into the vast global library and communication tool that is the internet'.

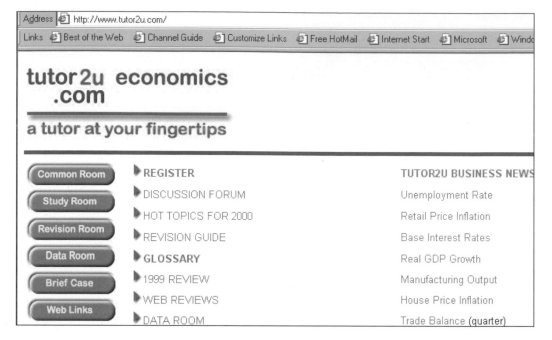

tutor2u economics .com

a tutor at your fingertips

Common Room	▶ REGISTER
Study Room	▶ DISCUSSION FORUM
Revision Room	▶ HOT TOPICS FOR 2000
Data Room	▶ REVISION GUIDE
Brief Case	▶ GLOSSARY
Web Links	▶ 1999 REVIEW
	▶ WEB REVIEWS
	▶ DATA ROOM

TUTOR2U BUSINESS NEWS

Unemployment Rate

Retail Price Inflation

Base Interest Rates

Real GDP Growth

Manufacturing Output

House Price Inflation

Trade Balance (quarter)

Fig. 10. Tutor2U Economics. If you teach economics, you will find this site useful. From its home page you can access ideas, support and information.

UK Schools on the Web (UK)
http://www.angliacampus.com/schools/
This database is hosted by Anglia Campus, a joint venture between BT and Anglia Multimedia. On this web site it maintains a comprehensive list of school web sites. You can choose from its alphabetical list of schools, separated into primary, secondary and others, or by regions using its clickable map. Some other schools are listed too. If you want to add your school to the list, or update your details, you can email them.

Welsh Secondary Schools (UK)
http://www.aber.ac.uk/ ~ dwj/wsecondsc.html
This is a useful web directory of Welsh secondary schools which have developed their own home pages. The information has been collected and presented by the Education Department at the University of Wales Aberystwyth. The site appears in both Welsh and English.

Further education

BBC Further Education Web Site (UK)
http://www.bbc.co.uk/education/fe/index.shtml
This site contains a wide range of online resources for all students and lecturers involved in Further Education. There's a complete guide to the full range of relevant BBC TV programmes, a growing collection of online activities, the new BBC *FE Newsletter* and more.

College Net (USA)
http://www.collegenet.com/
College Net is a portal for applying to colleges over the web in US, Canada, Africa, Europe and Mexico. There are links to online and distance

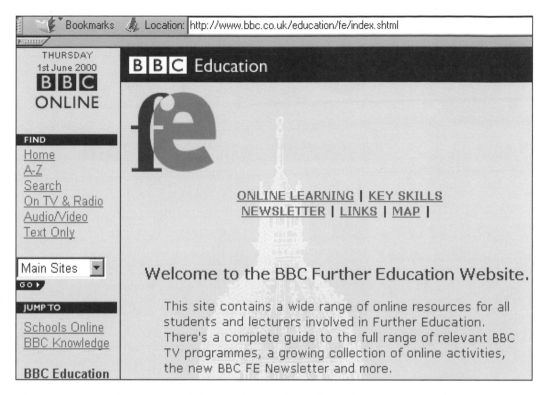

education colleges. You can search for a college by level of qualification, length of study or location. You can click on financial aid and scholarship buttons and there is a link to a virtual bookstore.

FE Colleges: University of Wolverhampton List & Maps (UK)
http://www.scit.wlv.ac.uk/ukinfo/felisth.html
A very useful database of UK further education colleges is maintained here at the University of Wolverhampton. You can link directly to the colleges from the list shown here, or explore a clickable map (undergoing revision). This is probably the best reference available.

Further Education Development Agency (UK)
http://www.feda/ac.uk/
The home page of the FEDA site has several icons. You can find updates, data on what's new and downloads. Newsdesk provides press releases and vacancy information. Under 'useful links' there are links to sites such as the National Grid for Learning. At 'products and services' you can access Training, a database of planned events and publications. The resource link takes you to the information centre, library, publications or the cybercentre. Under 'products and services', you have research and FEDA consultancy. Under programmes there are links to funding, GNVQ support programme, widening participation, regional services and international development.

Fig. 11. The BBC offers several excellent educational sites. Its own Further Education web site gives access to over 3,000 other web sites for learning.

Fig. 12. Oncourse is a useful gateway site to thousands of courses of all kinds in the UK, Europe and further afield.

Further Education Funding Council (UK)
http://www.fefc.ac.uk/index.html
The purpose of the FEFC is to secure further education provision that meets the needs and demands of individuals, employers and the requirements of government in respect of the location, nature and quality of provision. You can link into media releases, council news, circulars, college performance indicators and college inspection reports.

On Course (UK)
http://www.oncourse.co.uk/
On Course is designed to help you find the right course anywhere in the UK. Whether you're looking for languages in London, fashion in France or even a first job in finance, you could find it here.

Scottish Further Education Unit (UK)
http://www.sfeu.ac.uk/
The Unit contributes to the development of learning provision within FE colleges through the support of staff and the curriculum.

Learning resources

Choice in Education (UK)
http://www.choiceineducation.co.uk/
You can visit this site for the UK magazine (published monthly) for those who educate their children at home. It contains articles, legal guidelines, and information about support groups.

Hasslefree Learning (New Zealand)
http://www.hasslefree.co.nz
This site provides teachers and students with an interactive learning experience and an introduction to the world wide web.

Learnfree (UK)
http://www.learnfree.co.uk/
Through this snazzy-looking site, you can link into a treasure trove of information and links for all those involved in education: teachers, parents, pupils and students. It comes from the teachers' newspaper, the *Times Educational Supplement*.

Learn in Freedom (USA)
http://learninfreedom.org/
This site is all about taking responsibility for your own learning. It's about using your initiative to seek out learning, and using schools and teachers only if they are helpful to you, and voluntarily chosen by you. There are countless resources on and off the web to help you find the freedom to learn independently. Check the What's New Page for the latest additions to the site.

Learning Online from Anglia Multimedia (UK)
http://www.anglia.co.uk/angmulti/learning/
Teachers and students should find this an excellent curriculum resource on all the major learning subjects.

Learning to Teach Online (UK)
http://www.sheffcol.ac.uk/lettol/enquire.htm
The LeTTOL course was developed in the UK under the Further Education Development Agency's 'Quality in Information and Learning Technology' Programme, by the South Yorkshire Further Education Colleges' Consortium, a collaboration between all eight FE colleges in South Yorkshire. LeTTOL is for teachers, lecturers, trainers, materials developers, and academic or technical managers. It equips participants to teach and support learners online, manage online learning provision and apply appropriate learning methods in the design of on-line learning materials.

Microsoft in Education (USA)
http://www.microsoft.com/education/default.htm
'The Connected Learning Community is a simple yet powerful idea with even more relevance today than when we first introduced the concept five years ago. In our vision, new computing devices, powerful software, and the global explosion in web services combine to enable learning without limits – anytime, any place.' This site offers resources for teachers and educators. From the home page you can click onto instructional or technical resources, products, training, technology planning and partner opportunities. You can join the Microsoft Classroom Teacher Network or the Microsoft Mentor Program.

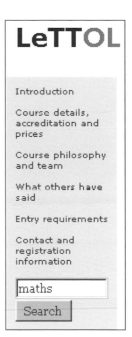

LeTTOL

Introduction

Course details, accreditation and prices

Course philosophy and team

What others have said

Entry requirements

Contact and registration information

maths

Search

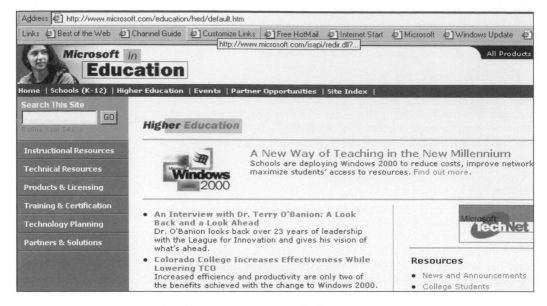

Fig. 13. Microsoft in Education. This site is specifically aimed at the education market. You can link into instructional resources for students and faculty development from here.

New Horizons for Learning (USA)
http://www.newhorizons.org/
NHL presents articles and information on educational issues. These include restructuring schools, technology in the classroom, arts in education, integrative education, adolescence, special needs, transition, inclusion, inclusive schools, inventive thinking, teaching problem solving, design of learning environments, inclusive classrooms, brain research and multicultural issues.

Online Educator (USA)
http://learnersonline.com/
Online Educator is a monthly print/electronic periodical which deals with educational resources on the net, online lessons. and online learning web site reviews.

Personal Tutors (UK)
http://www.personal-tutors.co.uk
This site offers private tuition for students sitting GCSE and A-level ex-

Fig. 14. Personal Tutors enables you to access tutors all over England, Scotland and Wales through their home page. The subjects covered range from primary to secondary school levels and sixth form.

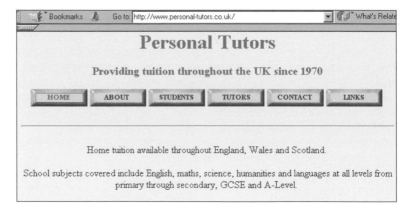

aminations including maths, English and the sciences. Based in Cheshire, it supplies tutors around the UK.

Sites Alive (USA)
http://www.sitesalive.com
From this breezy-looking web site you can link your classroom to real students at real field sites around the globe. Conservation and environmental issues are well represented.

Teaching and Learning on the World Wide Web (USA)
http://www.mcli.dist.maricopa.edu/tl/index.html
On this excellent page, you can access links to about 700 sites that are using internet technology for learning. It includes sites that offer courses delivered entirely over the web, to courses that offer specific activities related to a class assignment, and courses that offer class support materials over the web. It is well organised and presented, and includes a search facility. Well worth a look.

Tele-School Online (UK)
http://www.teleschool.org.uk
This site provides internet links between home and school. Its server was down when reviewed.

Think Quest (USA)
http://www.thinkquest.org/
Think Quest is an international academic competition for students aged 12 to 19. The students work in teams of two or three to produce sets of web pages as teaching and learning tools for use by teachers and students around the world. Over $1 million is awarded annually in scholarships and cash to the winning teams and their coaches and schools. The site includes a searchable library of over 1,000 student entries.

Treasure Island Teaching Unit (USA)
http://www.dreamcatchers.net/treasure
This site is a good example of an online teaching unit. It is based on Robert Louis Stevenson's classic novel, *Treasure Island*. It includes a seven-week programme of student activities and a schedule for teachers.

WWW.A-levels (UK)
http://homepages.tesco.net/ ~ richard.tarrant/cdl.htm
This site offers a useful collection of links for A-level students looking for revision help on the net. The site includes sections covering all the main subjects including English, maths and the sciences. It has been produced with the support of Oxford-based Young Enterprise, which has the backing of business sponsors.

Teachers and parents

EdWeb Home Room (USA)
http://edweb.cnidr.org/resource.cntnts.html
This site offers a guide put together by Andy Carvin, and is something of an experiment in online information and learning in exploring technology and school reform. There are links to educational resources and authoring, Andy's own presentations, and related educational resources.

Global SchoolNet Foundation (USA)
http://www.gsn.org/
This is a non-profit corporation which contributes to the philosophy, design, culture, and content of educational networking on the internet and in the classroom.

International Educators' Network Association (USA)
http://www.iteachnet.com/
This site is updated every day and is written by a team of international schoolteachers who have volunteered to make a useful resource for international schoolteachers and administrators, and others interested in international education. The home page presents a huge range of options including a webzine, bulletin boards, joining the association, professional development, curriculum issues, resources and specialist areas of interest, all of which can be accessed through a search.

Internet Schoolhouse (USA)
http://www.internetschoolhouse.com/
The Internet Schoolhouse is a virtual school formed to promote global friendship. Educators join because of its ease of use and friendly interface. The project offers a staff development book called *The Internet Schoolhouse: a Teacher's Best Friend,* designed to help teachers harness the vast power of the internet in an educational setting, and to suggest how lesson plans can be combined with the world wide web. It offers technology workshops, ranging from how to turn on a computer to training teachers in the use of the internet in the classroom. It provides opportunities for teachers to take part in and run classroom projects.

Judi Harris' 'Mining the Internet' columns
http://www.ed.uiuc.edu/Mining/Overview.html
From this site, you can access some useful articles from ISTE's 'Mining the Internet' series in *The Computing Teacher.* Some of them show educators how to design educational online activities. To complement these articles written by Judi Harris, you'll find examples of more than 200 network-based educational activities that she classifies into activity structures at http://www.ed.uiuc.edu/Activity-Structures/

National Confederation of Parent Teachers Associations (UK)
http://www.ncpta.org.uk/
The confederation represents 11,500 PTAs in England, Wales and Northern Ireland. It works to encourage 'the fullest co-operation between home

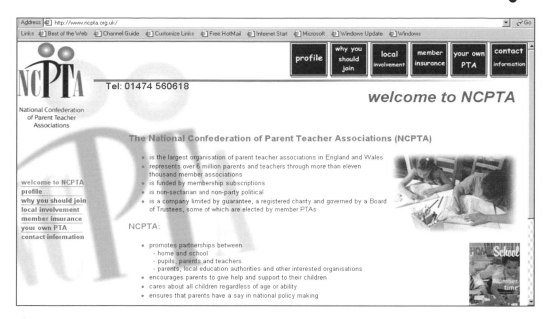

Fig. 15. The UK National Confederation of Parent Teachers Associations web site explains how you get involved locally, and even how you can start your own PTA.

and school, education authorities, central government and other interested parties and bodies'. The site explains how to join and participate.

National School Network (USA)
http://nsn.bbn.com
Through this site, you can link to a broad partnership of organisations working on building state-of-the-art applications for networking in education, including curriculum projects and online events.

OFSTED (UK)
http://www.ofsted.gov.uk/ofsted.htm
The Office of HM Chief Inspector of Schools in England sends inspectors to state schools and reports to the government. The site describes what they are supposed to do, and how they achieve it.

School and College Performance Tables (UK)
http://www.dfee.gov.uk/perform.htm
There are yearly statistics on performance and absenteeism in UK primary and secondary schools and colleges from the Department for Education and Employment on this site. See how your own school has done.

School Curriculum: a Brief Guide (UK)
http://www.dfee.gov.uk/schurric.htm
You can find out what every parent with a child in state schooling needs to know about the subjects taught in primary and secondary schools, how progress is assessed and what national tests are compulsory. There is also information on pupils' choices and parents' rights.

Teaching Web (Canada)
http://www.edu.yorku.ca/~rowston/chapter.html
This site contains an article written by Ron Owston on the value of the

web in education and published in *Educational Researcher*.

Teachnet.Com (USA)
http://www.teachnet.com/
From the home page of this site, you can access resources for teachers and other options. You can link to lesson ideas, reviews and resources. There are bulletin boards, activities, teacher-2-teacher and ePALS. You can link with Teachernet, sponsors and partners, and access the search facility.

Teachers Net (USA)
http://teachers.net/
You can access all kinds of features such as teacher chat, forums, news, and other resources through this substantial site. Its affiliates include Canadian Teachers.net and Australian.Teachers.net.

Teacherzone (USA)
http://www.teacherzone.com
This site offers resources and links for teachers. From a busy home page, you can click onto jobsearch, site index, lesson plans, resources for technology and the internet (including special needs), sponsorship, news, education software, web sites for and by kids, and contact points.

Fig. 16. Topmarks Education. Parents and teachers should find this site useful. It can even help you with creating your own educational web pages.

Topmarks Education (UK)
http://www.topmarks.co.uk/
From the home page, you can access a parents' area with articles written by practising teachers, for example on learning through play and ten tips on hearing your child read. The home page offers a teachers' area with teachers' resources and a schools-in-touch link. At the time of writing,

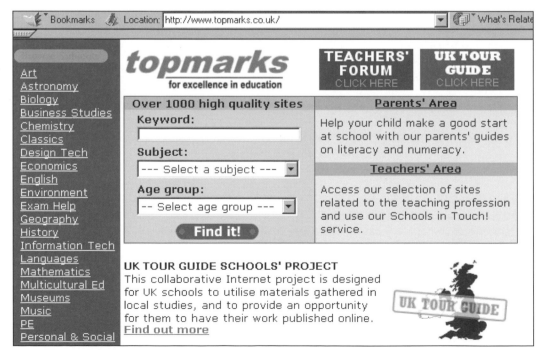

the 'star site' on the home page was Learning Curve, a site for history teachers and those studying GCSE history. There are browse subjects on the home page such as religious studies.

Welsh Joint Education Committee (UK)
http://www.wjec.co.uk/
On this simple WJEC home page, there is an introduction, a bookshop, MEU Cymru (Welsh software), the National Language Unit of Wales, examinations, a European unit, expressive arts and the Comenius Centre (three sites offering services to teachers and learners of modern foreign languages and Welsh). Also on the home page are a couple of press release options. You can read this site in Welsh or English.

World Wide Web in Education (USA)
http://edweb.cnidr.org/wwwedu.html
This is a moderated discussion service with over 1,600 members from 35 countries. You can use it to learn more about the organisation, to browse through the archive of past discussions, and to subscribe to the list itself. A simple home page offers access to subscription, browsing the discussion archive, and searching the archive. The site is maintained by EdWeb.

Educational technology

21st Century Teachers (USA)
http://www.21ct.org/
This volunteer initiative encourages 100,000 teachers to develop and share new skills for using technology in their teaching and learning activities. They range from the English teacher wanting to share innovative curriculum ideas with colleagues, to the science teacher helping students access science information over the internet, and to the third grade teaching assistant who using multimedia to create new learning opportunities. The initiative is supported by the University of Phoenix.

Classroom Connect Online (USA)
http://www.classroom.net/
This site works with educators in bringing the power of the internet to students. Clicking from the home page will take you to awards, jobs, contact points, partnerships and an online store.

Combined Higher Education Software Team (UK)
http://www.chest.ac.uk/
CHEST acts as a focal point for the supply of software, data, information, training materials and other IT related products to the higher and further education sectors. It also agrees educational discount prices for more than 1,000 products. It publishes an online CHEST Directory which is updated daily and freely available. Well worth exploring.

about
centres
news & events
publications
resources
search

Computers in Teaching Initiative (UK)
http://info.ox.ac.uk/cti/
Based at Oxford University Computing Services, this timely initiative

comprises 24 subject-based centres working to encourage the use of learning technologies throughout UK higher education.

CTI Courseware Databases (UK)
http://www.niss.ac.uk/education/cti/
This searchable and browsable facility provides information on software materials useful for teaching and learning. It covers accounting, finance and management, biology, the environment, chemistry, computing economics, engineering, geography, geology and meteorology, mathematics, sciences, modern languages, music, physics, psychology and other subjects. It is part of the Computers in Teaching Initiative (see above).

Education Communications (Canada)
http://www.educom.com/welcome.html
EduCom aims to integrate the internet and other forms of electronic communications into the education environment. It offers help with policy planning, programme development, internet or intranet communications, web site design, database creation with wide area access to the data, telecoms integration, and more.

Eduweb (UK)
http://www.eduweb.co.uk/
This is a project of the Oxford-based educational computer company Research Machines Ltd (RML). It includes a database of over 5,000 educational web pages, searchable by age range, subject and free text searching. School Web publishing gives you your own area in which to develop educationally relevant web pages. The At School directory is the largest UK directory of school, college and LEA web pages. It contains school newsletters, examples of pupils' work, photographs of foreign exchange trips and many other examples of imaginative internet publishing, all created by schools, colleges and individuals. Some parts of EduWeb are accessible only by premium service subscribers.

Heriot-Watt University Institute for Computer Based Learning (UK)
http://www.icbl.hw.ac.uk/
Here you can find out about research in computer-based learning and its impact on teaching and training.

Institute for Learning and Teaching (UK)
http://www.cti.ac.uk/links/ilthe/
You can find out more about the new higher education institute recommended by the Dearing Report.

International Telementor Center (USA)
http://www.telementor.org/
This is a program at the Center for Science, Mathematics & Technology Education at Colorado State University. It facilitates electronic mentoring relationships between professional adults and students worldwide. By spending 30 to 45 minutes a week communicating by email, adult mentors can share their experiences and expertise, helping students to

achieve academic excellence in maths and science, improve their communication skills, and explore career and educational options.

Internet Detective (UK)
http://sosig.ac.uk/desire/teachers.html
Internet Detective teaches generic internet and information skills, and can be used to support teaching and training in all kinds of educational settings. A Powerpoint presentation is available to introduce the Internet Detective tutorial to students.

Learning Space (USA)
http://www.learningspace.org/
Learning Space is for teachers, created by teachers, and about teachers. There are links to funding, technology, a teacher's lounge, global connections and video-conferencing, online tutorials, teacher resources, conferences, a Learning Space Intranet and membership.

Project Merlin (UK)
http://www.hull.ac.uk/langinst/merlin/
This is a collaborative research project with British Telecom. It aims to develop a distance learning environment using a combination of internet and telephone technology.

Technology Education Centre (UK)
http://www.technologyindex.com/education/index.html
This is an internet gateway, forum, and supplier of learning resources for students and teachers of technology.

Fig. 17. WWW4teachers offers an indexed collection of online resources created by teachers for teachers through this home page. Visit the webzine for information and entertainment.

Technology Teachers Association (UK)
http://www.sccc.ac.uk/tta
The TTA is an organisation founded in 1955 as a support group for fellow technical and technology teachers in Scotland.

WWW4teachers (USA)
http://www.4teachers.org/
The web site offers an indexed collection of online resources made by teachers for teachers. It includes web lessons, interviews, and discussions on using technology in education.

Related chapters

Chapter 4 – Vocational training web sites
Chapter 7 – Distance and online learning web sites
Chapter 8 – Specialist web sites for particular groups
Chapter 9 – Best of the rest

Related Internet Handbooks

The Internet for Schools, Barry Thomas & Richard Williams (Internet Handbooks).
Protecting Children on the Internet, Graham Jones (Internet Handbooks).

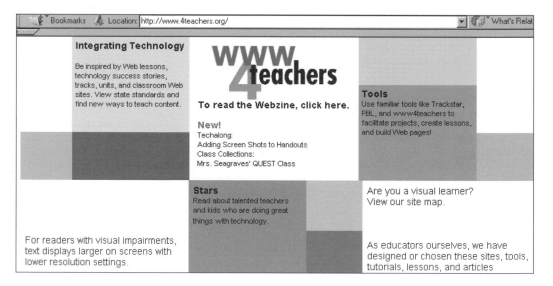

3 Higher education online

In this chapter we will explore:

▶ *higher education and the internet*
▶ *higher education links*
▶ *technology in higher education*
▶ *virtual higher education courses*

. . . .

Higher education and the internet

Universities across the country and the globe are rushing to build digital campuses and offer web-enabled distance learning. Electronic learning is the internet-based process by which students increase their knowledge and skills via electronic interaction.

The services of a 'virtual university' typically include:

1. electronic learning, mentoring and counselling
2. electronic registration and admissions
3. electronic advisory services
4. a digital library and an electronic bookstore
5. electronic co-curricular and student activities
6. electronic assessment of student learning.

The virtual university, parallel to and linked to the physical university, is the framework within which electronic learning takes place as a supplement to face-to-face courses, and where full certificate and degree programs are delivered and non-credit lifelong/continuing education courses and professional continuing education are electronically offered (both as a supplement to face to face non-credit offerings and as the mechanism for the full delivery of non-credit courses). It also provides the framework within which special electronic lectures can be offered. Further, the virtual university – using technologies such as computer conferencing and desktop video conferencing – helps provide the sense of 'virtual community' which enriches the electronic learning experience.

Web-based instruction
Web-based instruction (WBI) involves delivering course material, administering tutorials and quizzes or communicating with students. This also encompasses using the web to teach a class. There has been a dramatic increase in the level of interest and activity in WBI. Software writers are responding by creating software that facilitates the creation process and provides student management features. A number of these tools have evolved from computer-based training (CBT) software which are being 'retro-fitted' to work on the web. Others are brand new programs written from scratch to fill this role. While some commercial products are available, many of the current crop of programs were developed at universities by

instructors unable to find suitable off-the-shelf software. Most of the software, commercial and 'home-grown', is still in the development ('beta-testing') stage.

Once registered, students scan log on to the course homepage, enter a username and password, and access the course material. They can also use the email, newsgroup or 'live' chat functions to communicate with other students, the lecturer and markers for the course. Typically, these communication functions are available through the web page and are part of the software package. Students can also take online tutorials (with immediate feedback) as well as timed quizzes that are marked online. Once the course is finished, lecturers can update course material or make class announcements as needed. They can also make up tests and tutorials and administer them through the web. The software provides the facility to track the progress of students. Reports are available on which pages a particular student has accessed, as well as the number of times an individual page has been accessed by all students.

Higher education links

Association of University Teachers
http://www.aut.org.uk/
AUT is the trade union and professional body representing all types of professional staff across the UK higher education sectors.

BBC Learning Zone: Open University (UK)
http://www.bbc.co.uk/education/lzone/gen.shtml
This site offers support and links.

Commonwealth Universities Association
http://www.cwlthuniversitiesassoc.org.uk
This is the accrediting body for Commonwealth universities and colleges.

Euro Study Centres (European Union)
http://bridge.anglia.ac.uk/www/eurostudy.html
The Euro Study Centre network has centres providing information and services about higher education courses available through flexible learning packages.

Higher Education Funding Council for England (UK)
http://www.hefce.ac.uk/
The home page of this site offers contact points to HEFCE and click-on buttons to guide you around its site. There is a search function and site index on the home page. You can explore HEFCE background information, learning and teaching, finance, universities and colleges, publications, research, good practice, partners, news and events and questions.

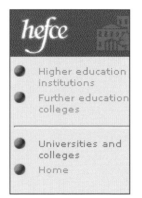

Higher Education in the Learning Society: The Dearing Report (UK)
http://www.leeds.ac.uk/educol/ncihe/
This web site hosts the full text of the report submitted to the Secretaries of State for Education and Employment, Wales, Scotland and Northern Ireland in July 1997. The report makes recommendations on how the

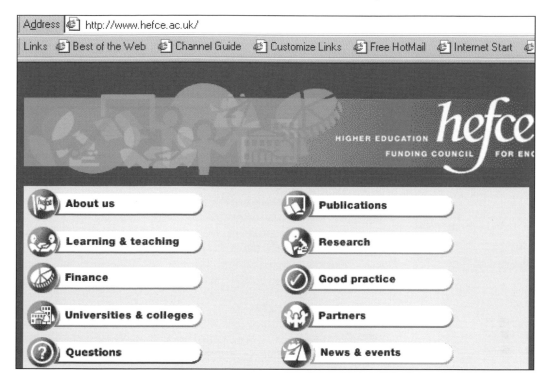

purposes, shape, structure, size and funding of higher education, including support for students, should develop to meet the needs of the UK over the next 20 years.

Internet2 Project
http://www.internet2.edu
This is the official site of a major project to meet academia's research and education requirements in the new century. Led by over 170 US universities working in partnership with industry and government, Internet2 is developing advanced network applications and technologies. Networking, authentication, authorisation and accounting will allow advanced applications to operate seamlessly among many organisations.

JANET (UK)
http://www.ja.net/
JANET is the network for the education and research community within the United Kingdom. It contains handy links to all the leading institutions of higher education in the UK. The JANET network and services are managed by UKERNA on behalf of the Joint Information Systems Committee (JISC). It is the UK point of contact for the Internet2 project.

Listing of all HE Institutions (UK)
http://www.hesa.ac.uk/links/he.inst.htm
Here you will find a very useful list of all UK universities with addresses, central phone numbers, fax numbers, chief officers and direct links. You can search by clicking onto an alphabetical letter and then scrolling down.

Fig. 18. The Higher Education Funding Council for England aims to promote good practice in learning and teaching in higher education. Visit the News and Research areas of its web site for the latest details.

Higher education online ....

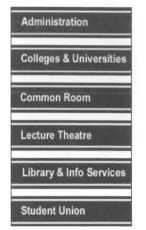

Administration

Colleges & Universities

Common Room

Lecture Theatre

Library & Info Services

Student Union

The site is maintained by HESA. There is a contact point for additions or amendments.

NISS (UK)
http://www.niss.ac.uk/
National Information Services & Systems provides a very useful gateway to UK universities, colleges and other academic sites. It is part of Edu-Serve, a not-for-profit company formed to operate the services of CHEST, NISS and Athens formerly hosted by staff of the Universities of Bath, Southampton and East Anglia.

Ortelius (Europe)
http://ortelius.unifi.it/ortelius/index2.html
This site offers a database on higher education in Europe. From the home page click on to institutes and courses (you need to subscribe to get into this one), institutional contracts, EU programmes, description of the national higher education systems, EU acts on higher education, and subscription details.

Peterson's Education (USA)
http://petersons.com/preview/votec.html
Here you can find details of over 7,500 US institutions of higher education which offer post-secondary awards, certificates, or diplomas requiring less than the two years study for an associate degree. The programs at these schools are career oriented. They are primarily in the fields of business: real estate, banking, accounting, technology, personal services, health care and trade. However, many are in more academic areas such as chemistry, library science, English language, and foreign language translation. Links include a bookstore and special schools, distance learning and contact points.

Sheffield NetLinkS (UK)
http://netways.shef.ac.uk/index.htm
Based in the Department of Information Studies, at the University of Sheffield, the NetLinkS project aims to encourage the development of networked learner support (NLS) by providing awareness-raising and professional development activities and resources. NetLinkS is a training and awareness project supported by the Higher Education Funding Council of England, as part of its electronic libraries programme.

TeleCampus (Canada)
http://telecampus.edu/
TeleCampus is a distributed distance learning centre. Its substantial database lists over 10,000 online courses from around the world. An online course is defined as one that can be taken on the internet from anywhere in the world. This ranges from a print-based correspondence course with email tutor support and submission of assignments, to an interactive web-based course. It does not include internet-based courses that have a residency requirement. Well worth exploring.

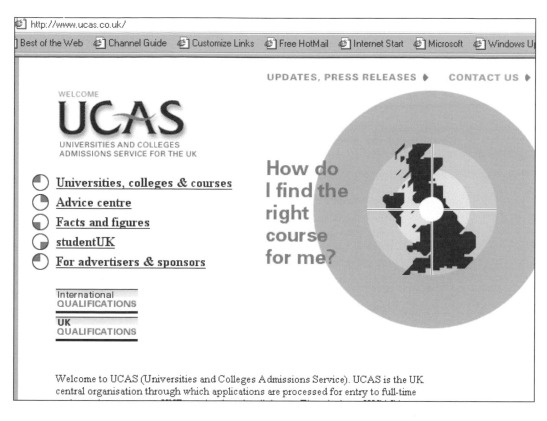

UPDATES, PRESS RELEASES ▶   CONTACT US ▶

WELCOME

UCAS

UNIVERSITIES AND COLLEGES
ADMISSIONS SERVICE FOR THE UK

- Universities, colleges & courses
- Advice centre
- Facts and figures
- studentUK
- For advertisers & sponsors

International
QUALIFICATIONS

UK
QUALIFICATIONS

How do
I find the
right
course
for me?

Welcome to UCAS (Universities and Colleges Admissions Service). UCAS is the UK
central organisation through which applications are processed for entry to full-time

UCAS (UK)

http://www.ucas.co.uk/

This site represents the Universities and Colleges Admissions Service for the UK, which processes applications for full-time undergraduate courses, Higher National Diplomas and university diplomas. This essential site includes general information about getting into a college or university, and links to the home pages of higher education institutions.

UK Academic Sites (UK)

http://src.doc.ic.ac.uk/uk-academic.html

This site offers an enormous range of UK universities and other academic sites giving links into their various departments. The opening page lists institutions in alphabetical order. Each link is maintained by the institution and offers course information including research and administration procedures. Some example links are the Open University, University of Brighton, and the Political Studies Association.

UK Higher Education Administrators (UK)

http://www.mailbase.ac.uk/juga/

Hosted by Mailbase, these pages have been designed to provide links of use to administrators in higher education. It includes complete A to Z lists of university and college web sites with hyperlinks.

Fig. 19. If you are looking for a place on a full-time undergraduate course, or to study for an HND or university diploma, visit the online service of UCAS, the universities and colleges admissions service. You can access both UK and international options from the home page.

UK Higher Education Student Unions Index (UK)
http://www.stu.uea.ac.uk/info/uksu.html
The home page of this enterprising site offers loads of links to student unions in most universities. Again from the home page, you can email the originators of the site to inform them of 'missing' sites or ones which should be listed and aren't. There is a link on the home page to Digital Networks Online where you can purchase hardware. The Union of UEA Students maintains this site and you can click on to a link on the home page to access their site.

UK Sensitive Maps (UK)
http://scitsc.wlv.ac.uk/ukinfo/uk.map.html
This excellent site is run by the University of Wolverhampton. It offers quick online access to higher education institutions. You can access their web sites via the map on the home page. By clicking onto the options on the left-hand side of the home page, you can access prospectuses for undergraduates and postgraduates, research, alumni, academic departments, library resources, information technology, students' unions, international students, profiles, admissions, teaching assessments, research assessments, search, directory, link list and contacts.

UKERNA
http://www.ukerna.ac.uk/
UKERNA is the United Kingdom Education & Research Networking Association. It manages the operation and development of the JANET networks under an agreement from the Joint Information Systems Committee (JISC) of the UK Higher and Further Education Funding Councils. Its key objectives are to: 'Take responsibility for the networking programme of the education and research community in the United Kingdom, and to research, develop and provide advanced electronic communication facilities for use in that community and in industry, thereby facilitating the extension of many classes of trade through its own and the community's links with industry.'

University Corporation for Advanced Internet Development (USA)
http://www.ucaid.edu/
UCAID is supported by over 175 member organisations: universities, corporations and non-profit organisations have joined to advance networking in higher education. Its activities include the Internet2 project, and programs devoted to network research, technology transfer, and collaborative activities in related fields such as distance learning and educational technology. Its projects include The Abilene Project that is developing a nationwide advanced network to serve as backbone network for the Internet2 project. Abilene will support the efforts of the over 130 universities working on the Internet2 project.

University of California at Berkeley (USA)
http://www.itp.berkeley.edu/WebResources.html
Berkeley's Instructional Technology Program maintains lists of worldwide web links that may be of interest to instructors.

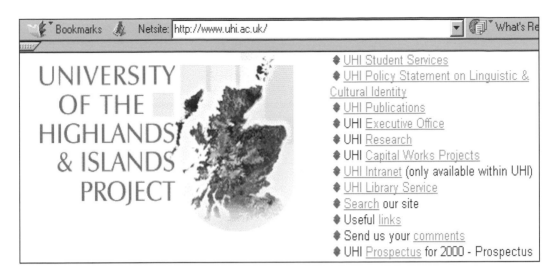

Netsite: http://www.uhi.ac.uk/

UNIVERSITY
OF THE
HIGHLANDS
& ISLANDS
PROJECT

♦ UHI Student Services
♦ UHI Policy Statement on Linguistic &
Cultural Identity
♦ UHI Publications
♦ UHI Executive Office
♦ UHI Research
♦ UHI Capital Works Projects
♦ UHI Intranet (only available within UHI)
♦ UHI Library Service
♦ Search our site
♦ Useful links
♦ Send us your comments
♦ UHI Prospectus for 2000 - Prospectus

University of the Highlands & Islands (UK)
http://www.uhi.ac.uk/
This site represents a consortium of twelve further education colleges
and research institutes collaborating on higher education projects and
research, including some options in open learning, distance learning,
online courses and courses at outreach centres.

Fig. 20. The University of
the Highlands & Islands
site is part of the UK
Millennium Project.

Unofficial Guides (UK)
http://www.unofficial-guides.com/
UG provides links to UK universities and student unions, as well as alternative information for prospective students.

Technology

Computers in Teaching Initiative (UK)
http://www.cti.ac.uk/
The CTI comprises 24 subject-based centres working to support the use
of communication and information technologies in UK higher education.
The CTI Support Service, which hosts this site, co-ordinates the work of
the centres and acts as a focal point for all CTI activities. The home page
gives you access to publications, resources, online news, search and
contacts.

Institute of Educational Technology (UK)
http://iet.open.ac.uk
This is a centre for the teaching, research and development of technology
in the service of student learning. The site is worked in collaboration with
Open University faculty and regional colleagues. From the home page
you can access courses (postgraduate, professional development, HE
teacher accreditation), research, projects, publications and consultancy.
There is a search facility.

Virtual higher education courses

▶ *Note* – This section provides links to a number of higher education courses which can be undertaken online. The vast majority of these are still American, the US being several years ahead of the rest of the world in pioneering online education. It would be impossible to list all these. A representative sample has therefore been included, together with details of UK and other institutions which have begun to develop virtual courses online. A major initiative is Internet2, a new version of the internet being specially evolved for academic use worldwide. It should be remembered that publicly funded institutions are not the only organisations in the world to describe themselves as 'universities'.

Athabasca University (Canada)
http://www.athabascau.ca
Athabasca is a Canadian Open University offering a Master of Distance Education program with a primary focus on the fields of distance education and training. All courses for the degree are delivered using distance education media, including the internet. There are no face-to-face requirements for completing a degree. From the home page you can access student services, the library, courses, and a search facility.

Athena Academy give

Athena University (USA)
http://www.athena.edu/
This non-profit institution is a virtual online university. It has established a virtual education environment (VEE) on the internet and can be accessed inexpensively from anywhere on the globe. It provides a forum in which students and teachers can pursue an integrated, interdisciplinary curriculum in the liberal arts.

Boise State University (USA)
http://ivc.idbsu.edu/
Idaho Virtual Campus at Boise State is training and educating university instructors to design more interactive courses, using internet technology. In the first year it made three university courses – introductory astronomy, planetary geology, and earth systems science – fully accessible to off-campus learners.

Bradford University (UK)
http://www.brad.ac.uk/
Bradford University has devised what appears to be the UK's first online university business studies course using video teaching and email in place of traditional tutorials (September 1999). Students can use a web site to enrol, pay fees and study for the course, which begins in September. 'People from all over the world can now study at Bradford without leaving their armchair. They could sit at the South Pole or in the jungle and study at Bradford if they had the technology. There's no limit to the number of students who can sign up for the course. We can put people into different email seminar groups. People will be able to talk to the tutors

through email. There will also be pre-recorded video lectures which will be delivered worldwide.'

Brigham Young University (USA)
http://coned.byu.edu/is/index.htm
BYU offers university and high school courses completely online for full university or high school credits. Lecture materials, internet links, video and audio clips, assignments, and grades are all available online.

California Virtual University (USA)
http://www.california.edu/
This site ties together the online and distance learning course offerings from colleges and universities across California. The Virtual University Foundation includes the state's main university systems, the University of California, California State University, and California Community College organisations, and several top corporations including Sun, Cisco Systems, Pacific Bell, International Thomson Publishing, and Oracle. CVU offers students 1,600 courses entirely online.

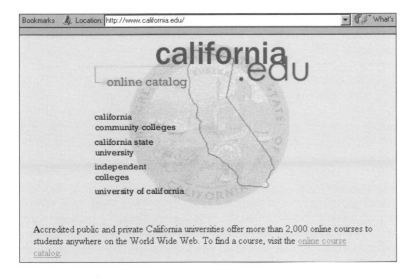

Fig. 21. California Virtual University is a portal to Californian universities. You can find out about all kinds of distance and online courses from this page.

Carleton University (Canada)
http://vv.carleton.ca/
This site runs Virtual Ventures, a non-profit student organisation that operates fun and exciting computer education programs for youth. The program is maintained through the Department of Engineering at Carleton University.

CASO's Internet University (USA)
http://www.caso.com/
CASO's New Promise project aims to help students and teachers make sense of the revolution in education that is taking place on the internet. It is designing tools to help educators make informed decisions concerning the courses and schools to choose. Use the site to find a college course

that can be taken online, get counselling on online education, and to get a degree online. You can search its course database by category or by institution.

Christopher Newport University (USA)
http://cnuonline.cnu.edu/
Christopher Newport University is a coeducational, state-supported institution within Virginia's public university system. The university is organised, and instruction provided, to meet the life-long learning interests and needs of a largely part-time and mobile student body. Its classes are based on the use of WebCT.

City University, Washington (USA)
http://www.cityu.edu/
City University is a private, non-profit institution of higher education. It was founded to serve working adults who want to build on their education but cannot interrupt their careers to become full-time students. Its Online Instructional Centre shows how to find and complete certain courses via the internet. There is a wide choice of courses in social studies, business management, law, computer science, and study skills. Some of the web pages are loaded with graphics and can be slow to compile.

Clyde Virtual University (UK)
http://cvu.strath.ac.uk/
Clyde began as a test-bed for exploring, developing and evaluating techniques for delivering learning materials, supporting collaborative learning and carrying out assessment over the internet. The Virtual University includes a lecture theatre containing web-based courseware in a number of subject areas. There is a virtual library holding study material, links to physical libraries within the ClydeNet institutions, and courseware covering information and study skills. Visit the online administration office to register and find out more. There is a virtual cafe – you supply the coffee, they supply the chat. At the CVU online assessment hall, students can take tests either as part of an interactive courseware module or as stand-alone assessments.

CMN Virtual University (USA)
http://www.menominee.com/vu.htm
The College of the Menominee Nation Virtual University is controlled by native American Indians and offers a variety of programs. In addition to a two-year technical degree, it offers 2+2 programs where students begin their education at CMN and go on to the University of Wisconsin system to earn a four-year degree in a variety of fields. The site presents the courseware that CMN is currently offering, using the internet as its delivery medium.

Colorado Electronic Community College (USA)
http://www.cecc.cccoes.edu
CECC runs Associate of Arts and Associate of Science degrees through

distance learning technology involving cable, video, CD-rom, the internet, PictureTel, voicemail and other electronic and distance learning methods.

Colorado State University (USA)
http://www.biz.colostate.edu/
This site offers an MBA program in which most of the required course-work is completed using the internet. Asynchronous interaction with the faculty and other classmates can take place using any number of re-sources available to students – the internet, world wide web, fax, or telephone. Each student in the program must have access to a computer and to the internet.

Columbia Pacific University (USA)
http://www.itstime.com/cpu/default.htm
This site provides higher education with holistic emphasis for accom-plished adults, whose goals are undergraduate or graduate degrees in arts and sciences, administration and management, or health and human services.

Comforce University Virtual Campus
http://university.comforce.com/
Comforce is a commercial provider of staffing and outsourcing solutions for the high-tech world. Through its home page, you can access courses ranging from the latest releases of desktop applications and software packages to general management and communications skills training.

Courses Online (Canada)
http://www.unb.ca/web/wwwdev/c3.html
This site is maintained by the University of New Brunswick. It contains a compilation, by subject matter, of online courses and other web-based materials, plus information of interest to people developing courseware to be delivered in part or totally over the web.

CyberEd University
http://www3.umassd.edu/
CyberEd offers a selection of standard, full-credit university courses to the global audience of the web through the University of Massachusetts Dartmouth Division of Continuing Education. Their objective is to create a distance learning environment that rivals the traditional classroom envir-onment in quality and content of learning experience.

Deakin University (Australia)
http://www.deakin.edu.au/
Here you can link into Deakin courses which are offered completely online to students anywhere in the world.

Digital U (Canada)
http://www.digital-u.com/
Based in Vancouver, Digital U offers ways of exploring, experiencing and learning about the latest computer technology in a hands-on environ-

Fig. 22. Digital U is a cyber cafe with attitude. The home page offers access to what's new at Digital U, and to a free email service.

ment. At Digital U you can explore the internet, and try out hundreds of software programs.

Diversity University
http://www.du.org/
DU is a non-profit organisation dedicated to promoting education through online services. Its main interest is developing virtual reality educational environments, and other games, educational and role-playing environments.

Edith Cowan University Virtual Campus Australia (Australia)
http://www.cowan.edu.au/
ECU offers courses in arts, business, education, health and human sciences, science, technology and engineering, and the visual and performing arts from undergraduate to doctorate level. Its Virtual Campus network is a computer-based communications facility that gives students the electronic equivalent of on-campus services, accessible through their own home computer. Students are able to post mail to each other and to staff, submit assignments, call up library catalogues, read notice boards, submit and receive files of work, explore remote databases and the world wide web, and engage in real-time conversations with others on the system. Users can 'enter' the campus at any time, allowing 'just in time support' for their education programmes.

Electronic University Network (USA)
http://www.pangaeanetwork.com/colleges.html
The EUN is a network of accredited college and university education offered entirely online. It was founded in 1984 with the goal of helping colleges and universities to reach and teach students online. Its first group of universities launched their online courses in 1986. In 1992 it became the higher-education coordinator for America Online. The organisation

turned its attention to helping colleges and universities to develop, launch, and manage full degree programs, and the required courses, on their virtual campuses on AOL. From 1992 to 1997 ten additional institutions joined the EUN and offered courses and full degrees via AOL.

FernUniversität (Germany)
http://www.fernuni-hagen.de/
Fern is an autonomous institution and an integral part of the existing and recognised university system with equal rights and functions in teaching and research and offering high quality university study programmes. There is a short description in English.

Graduate School of America (USA)
http://www.tgsa.com/
This is a distance learning graduate school based in Minneapolis, Minnesota. It offers Master of Science (MS) and Doctor of Philosophy (PhD) degrees in Management, Education, Human Services, and Interdisciplinary Studies. Its curriculum is designed for working professionals and combines faculty-mentored distance learning with online course options.

Goteborg Virtual University (Sweden)
http://www.vu.gu.se/
Goteborg University is developing a virtual university to pioneer new methods and equipment in online education and lecturing. The text of the site is in Swedish.

Grad Schools (USA)
http://www.gradschools.com/
This is a useful online directory of programs, arranged by distance and conventional learning, in easy-to-use directories organised by curriculum.

Fig. 23. Grad Schools is another useful portal site. It contains more than 50,000 program listings and can be read in several different languages.

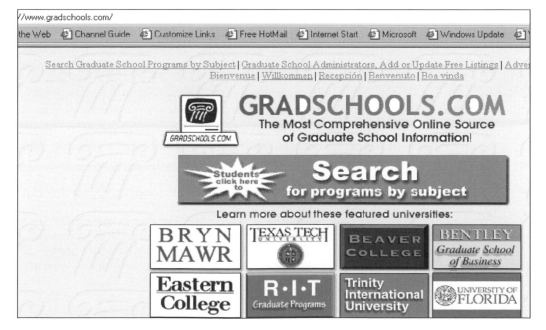

programmes
On-Campus MBA
Distance Learning MBA

Heriot Watt University (UK)
http://www.hwmba.edu/Programmes/dl.mba.over.htm
Its distance-learning MBA programme can be completed anywhere in the world. It is suited to individuals unprepared to take time away from work and family, or whose work requires them to travel extensively. Study materials are self-sufficient and there is no requirement for tutor or student contact.

Indiana Wesleyan Virtual University (USA)
http://doxie.indwes.edu/
This site offers electives in computing, earth science, biblical literature, English and multiple intelligence. The university also offers MBAs in research and technology, accounting, economics, statistical analysis and managing business information systems.

Israel's Open University (Israel)
http://www.openu.ac.il/
This is a distance education university designed to offer academic studies to students throughout Israel. Its home study method allows students all over the country to pursue a higher education, whenever and wherever convenient, without interfering with their other personal and vocational obligations. The text is in Hebrew and English.

La Trobe University (Australia)
http://chinese.bendigo.latrobe.edu.au
LaTrobe, at Bendigo, offers internet-based Chinese teaching and learning. You can browse the details of its online introduction, sample some actual Chinese lessons, and explore the links. The site explains how the tutorial is arranged, how to obtain an offline version of your online lessons, how to view the direct Chinese texts, and how to listen to the sound files. Each enrolled student is provided with a tutor for learning assistance, and all questions from the student must be emailed to the tutor responsible for academic inquiries. General tutorial material is published in its online *Chinabit Weekly* magazine. To view the direct Chinese texts you need to install a Chinese system with your web browser, and the site enables you to do this.

Long Island University Virtual Classrooms (USA)
http://phoenix.liu.edu/
Long Island University Virtual Classrooms is a partial list of course materials available over the internet.

Michigan State Virtual University (USA)
http://vu.msu.edu/
Virtual University is a name used at Michigan State University to refer to courses and instructional programs offered through the internet and other technologically enhanced media. These new technologies make it possible for MSU to offer instruction without the time and place constraints of traditional university programs.

Northland Polytechnic Virtual University (New Zealand)
http://www.northland.net.nz/virtualuni.htm
The virtual university is a project of the Northland Polytechnic and iGRIN
to create a new educational standard for the new century.

Northwestern State University (USA)
http://www.nsula.edu/
This site offers online registration and online courses as well as mainstream programs. Easy menu-type access from the home page takes
you everywhere (information, colleges and departments and clubs and
centres).

Open Learning Institute (Hong Kong)
http://www.oli.hk/
This Kowloon-based institute was set up by the Hong Kong government
in 1989. It is 'open', and was the first institution in Hong Kong to provide
higher education mainly through distance learning.

Open University: Knowledge Media Institute (UK)
http://kmi.open.ac.uk/
'KMi Stadium' is the generic label for a suite of activities and software
tools that have been evolving since mid-1995 at the OU's Knowledge
Media Institute. The common goal of these activities is to stage large-
scale live events and on-demand-replays, while giving remote participants anywhere on the internet a sense of 'being there'.

Open University (Netherlands)
http://www.ouh.nl
The OU of the Netherlands is an independent government funded institution for open higher distance education, established in 1985. The Dutch
government's purpose was to make higher education accessible to
anyone with the necessary aptitudes and interests, regardless of formal
qualifications. Its charter identifies two further aims: to create a more
cost-effective form of higher education, and to encourage innovation in
higher education, in terms of both curriculum and teaching methods. The
site is offered in English and Dutch.

Open University (UK)
http://www.open.ac.uk/
The OU is Britain's largest and most innovative university. Founded by
Royal Charter in 1969, it has grown rapidly both in student numbers and
range of courses. There are professional development programmes in
management, education, health and social welfare, manufacturing and
computer applications, as well as self-contained study packs.

Polytechnic Virtual University (USA)
http://pride-i2.poly.edu/virtual/
This is a New York-based 'virtual poly'. All its enrolled students are entitled
to free access to the internet, are given email accounts and can have their
own home pages on the world wide web. 'The Polytechnic Research

Institute for Development and Enterprise (PRIDE) has been building a new tool for education on the Internet. The Internet-Cyberspace Assisted Responsive Education (I-CARE) system is a comprehensive education solution for delivering a wide variety of courses over the internet, and can act as a test bed for the development of new academic strategies as this fundamental shift in educational paradigms progresses.'

PricewaterhouseCoopers Virtual University
http://www.vu.pw.com/
This is Pricewaterhouse Coopers' computer-based training service for various enterprise resource planning (ERP) packages such as SAP, Oracle and PeopleSoft.

Robert Gordon University (UK)
http://www.rgu.ac.uk/
This site has a virtual campus with access to NetLearn. It offers internet learning resources using downloadable material, non-computer based materials, email, and web-based material. It also offers teaching resources and other special resources, for example for the visually impaired.

Sacred Heart University
http://www.sacredheart.edu/distancelearning
This site offers online university credit courses, including English, business, chemistry, computer, and other subjects.

EXPLORE
Cool Zone
Free Zone
Chat Cafe
Bookstore
Help Desk

Simon Fraser University (USA)
http://virtual-u.cs.sfu.ca/vuweb/
Simon Fraser Virtual University aims to establish a framework for providing online educational resources by developing intelligent software tools enabling instructors to organise learning where student interaction is via computers in their business, education, or home environments.

Spectrum Virtual University
http://www.vu.org/
Spectrum claims that its virtual campus on the world wide web is the largest online learning community on the internet with more than half a million people from 128 countries having attended its online classes. The site contains starting points to explore its virtual campus: click the subscribe button to request the class calendar and campus newsletter. To sign up for classes, click the enrol button. Visit the Chat Cafe for real-time chat with VU students and alumni from around the world. If you've already enrolled, you'll find a personalised menu with links to your classes on Your Desk.

Sukhothai Thammathirat Open University (Thailand)
http://www.stou.ac.th/index.htm#Contents
Based in Nonthaburi, Thailand, STOU adheres to the principle of lifelong education. It aims at improving the quality of life of the public in general, seeks to increase the educational qualifications of working people, and strives to expand educational opportunities for secondary school gradu-

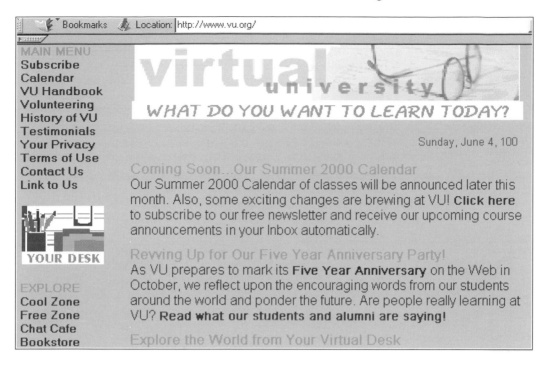

MAIN MENU
Subscribe
Calendar
VU Handbook
Volunteering
History of VU
Testimonials
Your Privacy
Terms of Use
Contact Us
Link to Us

YOUR DESK

EXPLORE
Cool Zone
Free Zone
Chat Cafe
Bookstore

WHAT DO YOU WANT TO LEARN TODAY?

Sunday, June 4, 100

Coming Soon...Our Summer 2000 Calendar
Our Summer 2000 Calendar of classes will be announced later this month. Also, some exciting changes are brewing at VU! **Click here** to subscribe to our free newsletter and receive our upcoming course announcements in your Inbox automatically.

Revving Up for Our Five Year Anniversary Party!
As VU prepares to mark its **Five Year Anniversary** on the Web in October, we reflect upon the encouraging words from our students around the world and ponder the future. Are people really learning at VU? **Read what our students and alumni are saying!**

Explore the World from Your Virtual Desk

ates. To reach these goals, it has established a distance-teaching system using correspondence media, radio and television programs and other methods, which enable students to study on their own without having to enter a conventional classroom.

TheU
http://www.ccon.org/theu/index.html
Here you can access a world virtual university project. It lies between traditional campus-based universities and the growing number of distance-learning projects. Distance learning using current methodology offers advantages to students in remote areas and students attending part-time courses.

United States Distance Learning Association
http://www.usdla.org/
The USDLA is a non-profit organisation formed in 1987. Its purpose is to promote the development and application of distance learning for education and training. The constituents it serves include Pre-K through to grade 12 education, higher education, home school education, continuing education, corporate training, military and government training, and telemedicine.

University Access Virtual Campus
http://www.universityaccess.com/
UA is a commercial internet/distance learning company established in 1996. Focusing on management education, training and knowledge, it aims to improve the online learning experience as the world progressively

Fig. 24. Spectrum Virtual University. From the home page of this site you can visit the Chat Café, the bookstore and the Cool Zone.

becomes a knowledge-based economy. Its courses are being taken by more than 3,000 students and 125 undergraduate, graduate, and corporate institutions US-wide. Its affiliates include several top international business schools such as the London Business School.

University of London External Programme
http://www.lon.ac.uk/external/
If you are looking for an undergraduate or postgraduate qualification without physically coming to the University of London, you can do it here. You can see an overview of all the degrees on offer, and either download a prospectus or order one by post. From the home page you can access and download parameters relating to each degree. There is a section for Q&As and contacts.

Fig. 25. The University of London External Programme. If you would like to study for a London degree without ever travelling to London, visit this site and explore its prospectus.

Bookmarks   Netsite: http://www.lon.ac.uk/external/

External Programme
University of London

Introduction   The University Colleges

Information for institutions

Exam
timetables
2000

Study for a
London degree without coming to London

The External Programme
The Information Centre , University of London, Malet Street, London WC1E 7HU United Kingdom
Tel: +44 (0)20 7862 8360/8361

Main index · Prospectus · Regulations · Answers to questions · Contacts

University of Maryland University College (USA)
http://nova.umuc.edu/distance/
UMUC offers a bachelor's degree at a distance in eight career-related specialisations including computer and information science and management. Selected graduate courses are also available. Enrolment is open to US citizens worldwide.

University of Missouri Kansas City (USA)
http://vu.umkc.edu/
This web site of UMKC supports VU courses and provides supplementary

material for campus-based courses. A VU course is one that can be taken from a remote location. Some campus-based courses also use the VU web site to distribute supplementary material and to facilitate discussions. The courses cover music, computer science, and adult education.

University of Ohio (USA)
http://iws.ohiolink.edu/
This site gives access to a special edition of the Ohio Link small grant research program, which has helped create 18 instructional web sites at Ohio campuses. These cover biology, electronics, engineering, English, marketing, medicine, philosophy, psychology, and more.

University of Technology (Australia)
http://www.uts.edu.au
This is a colourful, graphic and slow-loading site. From the home page you can access directly or by search contacts, information resources, courses, virtual open days, staff development and research.

University of Sheffield (UK)
http://www.shef.ac.uk/uni/projects/csnl/
This site represents the Centre for the Study of Networked Learning and the development of online courses. It is a useful place to keep up to date on UK developments in this field.

University of South Africa
http://www.unisa.ac.za/
This is one of the largest distance-teaching universities in the world. It affords equal education and employment opportunities to qualified persons regardless of race, colour, religion, gender, national origin, age,

Fig. 26. The University of South Africa offers internationally recognised certificates, diplomas and degrees up to doctorate level. This is its internet service, Students Online.

Bookmarks   Netsite: https://sol.unisa.ac.za/   ▼   What's Rel

Welcome to **Students On-line**, a service for registered Unisa students to get access to administrative and academic services via the Internet.

The system is being expanded to include most of the services that are normally done via mail or by visiting the campus.

Before you **ENTER SOL** for the first time, you have to **APPLY** to become a SOL user.

Please Note!
The Student Database will be down for maintenance for most of the weekend of 10 - 11 June 2000. Submission of assignments will not be possible during this time. We apologise for any inconvenience caused.

ENTER SOL	USER REGISTRATION
SOL HOURS	STATISTICS
FREQUENTLY ASKED QUESTIONS (FAQ)	EXAMINATION RESULTS
A TOUR OF SOL	STUDY INFORMATION
DISCUSSION FORUMS	UNISA NEWS

handicap, ancestry, place of birth, marital status, political affiliation or domicile.

University of Texas: World Lecture Hall (USA)
http://www.utexas.edu/world/lecture/
From the home page, you can visit the World Lecture Hall to see how its faculty members worldwide are using the web to deliver course materials.

Virginia Tech Virtual University (USA)
http://ebbs.english.vt.edu/
Virginia Tech has been building foundations of a virtual university since 1993 with its support for the Blacksburg Electronic Village, a state-wide broadband ATM network, the Faculty Development Initiative and the Cyber School project in the College of Arts and Sciences. The site contains information on web-based courses at Virginia Tech, online courses around the country, and electronic classes and resources.

Virtual Online University Services International (USA)
http://www.vousi.com/
VOUSI offers a commercial approach to delivering academic excellence, professional development and lifelong learning. It has developed an online interactive MBA program and 'corporate university' service. It uses an enhanced virtual education environment (VEE) as its electronic campus. A VEE allows one-on-one collaboration, debate, and interaction between fellow students and instructors using an innovative model for distance education.

Virtual University (USA)
http://www.vu.org/campus.html
Los Angeles-based Virtual University is a non-profit community which provides online learning and social support. It offers a database of resources and information. From the home page you can access a help facility, the bookstore as well as the full course range. Over half a million people from 128 countries have attended classes by using its virtual campus.

Virtual University Gazette (USA)
http://www.geteducated.com/vugaz.htm
The *Virtual University Gazette* is a free monthly email newsletter for distance learning professionals working in adult and post-secondary education and training. Each issue includes news of new distance learning programs in the academic and corporate sectors as well as job opportunities and links to online learning hot spots in the virtual university movement. VUG is published by Vicky Phillips, CEO of Lifelong Learning, a distance learning consulting firm located in Vermont.

Virtual University Pennsylvania (USA)
http://business.ship.edu/vu/
Virtual University is an alliance of Millersville University, Shippensburg University and West Chester University in south central Pennsylvania. It

offers various undergraduate and graduate courses for degree and non-degree students through distance learning technology.

Virtue (Norway)
http://www.virtue.uib.no/
Göteborg University, the University of Bergen, and the University of Maryland have joined together in the Virtue program to promote lifelong learning, public outreach, innovative communication technology, and international degree programs, as well as establish an international virtual university with open and strong partnerships between academia, industry, and government organisations. The project is concerned with global environmental and sustainability issues.

Walden University (USA)
http://www.waldenu.edu
Based in Minneapolis, Walden runs graduate study courses in the social sciences for busy adults who desire an advanced degree but can't forego career and personal commitments while they earn it. Its flexible delivery formats allow students to earn a master's or doctorate from the convenience of their home or workplace, uninterrupted by schedule or location.

Washington State University College (USA)
http://www.vpds.wsu.edu/
The College's Virtual Professional Development School has created a computer-based virtual classroom that helps incoming freshers to master the research and writing skills needed in college. The system allows students to do research using multimedia tools and the web, and collaborate with each other and with the faculty. Students can access their courses via the web from the computer labs on campus or from their dorm rooms or apartments. Using the environments WSU customised for Web University, students can interact in real time with other students in a chat-room style environment, or they can work on an assignment or an exam in an asynchronous manner.

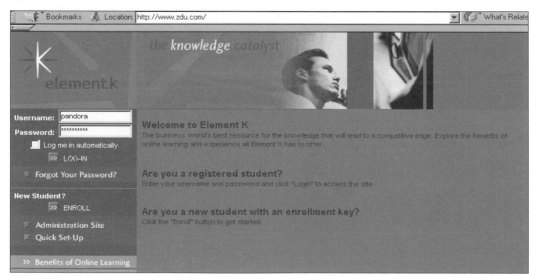

Higher education online ....

World University Online
http://www.worlduonline.com/Courses.htm
WUO is an independent commercial organisation that offers free online courses, tests, and hosting for student groups. It is dedicated to making education accessible to every person in an interesting way through a continual, interactive and personalised learning experience.

ZD Net University
http://www.zdu.com
Ziff-Davis is a leading media and marketing company focused on computing and internet-related technologies. It is one of the world's leading publishers of computer training materials. This site offers a 'total corporate online university'. Online computing classes and seminars are taught on private, moderated message boards. The courses on offer include C++, Intro to Java Applets, Beginning Delphi, and many others.

Related chapters

Chapter 4 – Vocational training web sites
Chapter 5 – Occupational training web sites
Chapter 7 – Distance and online learning web sites

Related Internet Handbooks

Graduate Job Hunting on the Internet, Laurel Alexander (Internet Handbooks).
Studying English on the Internet, Wendy Shaw (Internet Handbooks).
Studying Law on the Internet, Stephen Hardy (Internet Handbooks).
The Internet for Students, David Holland (Internet Handbooks).

4 Vocational training sites

In this chapter we will explore:

▶ *vocational training resources*

▶ *technology*

▶ *management training and development*

▶ *vocational education and training around the world*

▶ *UK qualifications awarding bodies*

▶ *online vocational courses*

▶ *vocational training links*

▶ *training for business owners*

▶ *research centres and government offices*

. . . .

Introduction

There are thousands of vocational training sites for the UK, let alone the rest of the world. There are sites for everyone, and sites for a wide range of occupational training. You can focus on training in the UK or go online with an American university. The permutations are endless for vocational training on the web.

Vocational training may, or may not be, qualification-led. There are vocational training providers offering public courses where staff from several different companies can attend or vocational training can be provided on a bespoke basis for a company. Individuals and companies can access vocational training opportunities. The best part of the internet is the increasing flexibility of how vocational training is delivered.

Fig. 27. Using the search engine Yahoo! to track down web sites dealing with vocational training.

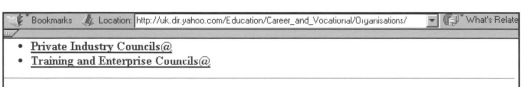

Bookmarks   Location: http://uk.dir.yahoo.com/Education/Career_and_Vocational/Organisations/   What's Relate

- **Private Industry Councils@**
- **Training and Enterprise Councils@**

- Big Trip 🏴 - helps young people considering the option of starting their own business.
- Independent Schools Careers Organisation (ISCO) 🏴 - offers careers and higher education guidance services, publications, careers magazine, and more.
- Industrial Careers Foundation 🏴 - aims to introduce students to the challenge of a career in management and to increase understanding between business and education.
- Prince's Trust 🏴 - helps provide opportunities for young people.

- National Council for Occupational Education **NEW!** - nonprofit organisation committed to promoting excellence in occupational education.

- American Vocational Association - professional non-profit organisation with a diverse array of programmes that advance vocational-technical and school-to-careers education.
- Apprenticeship Traineeship Services (ATS) - streamlined service which can provide information and assistance to current and prospective apprentices and trainees, and employers.

As companies continue to downsize and the work force grows more transient, it is becoming harder for companies to implement vocational training programmes. However, vocational training can be delivered in a number of flexible ways: direct training, distance learning, self-study, on-the-job coaching, open learning or online learning.

If you are an employer, your priorities are making and saving costs. Your core workforce may be small and your freelance base large. You may have a highly transient workforce. You may have a large number of part-time staff. All the nuances of flexible working can make it difficult to invest in staff training. You could rely on staff coming to you already well trained. Or you could provide a guiding hand in shaping your staff's potential through flexible learning – which you can find out about via your PC and the internet.

If you are a vocational trainer, you may find this chapter of use in finding work, updating your knowledge and skills, and networking. Guidance workers, careers officers and Employment Service staff will find this chapter invaluable in providing quick information across the vast field of vocational training. Those wanting to gain or improve their working-related skills can use this chapter to surf the net for flexible ways of learning that won't interfere with other commitments.

Because of the global marketplace, increased competition and more sophisticated technology, the world of work demands a high level of knowledge and skill. The message is slowly filtering through that each of us is responsible for our own learning curve. We need to be ready to reskill ourselves, and not to rely on the parent company to do it for us. This chapter offers links to vocational sites for everyone. Whether you are a guidance or HR professional working with clients who need work-related skills and qualifications, or whether you are looking for your own professional development – you should find the reviewed sites of interest.

Vocational training resources

American Society for Training and Development (USA)
http://www.astd.org/
ASTD actually has plenty to offer trainers working outside the US. Its site provides a substantial gateway to many articles and research reports, and you can find out about the world's the biggest training exhibition conference.

The Biz (UK)
http://www.thebiz.co.uk/
This Business Information Zone site is a UK business directory offering access to a virtual training zone which links you to The Virtual Training Calendar (training courses) or The Virtual Training Library (products). There is a search function that takes you into pages of further links related to your chosen area. For each title you will find pricing details, a short description of the product or service and an enquiry form for further information.

Electronic Training Village (Europe)
http://www.trainingvillage.gr/
This substantial site, which is a project of CEDEFOP, deals with vocational training information and research in Europe. Free registration is required to access the site fully. You can apply to be included in the Village *Who's Who in VET in Europe*.

Fenman (UK)
http://www.fenman.co.uk/
This site offers print-based and video-based training resources, from a publisher of materials for professional trainers. You can link into downloads, becoming an author, a catalogue, and learning sites.

Financial Times Management (UK)
http://www.ftmanagement.com/
FT Knowledge (a Pearson company) is one of the world's leading providers of business education and management development. Its Corporate Development division offers solutions to a wide range of development needs. Their library of off-the-shelf training products includes videos and multimedia titles. You can link into distance learning, degrees, and training and development.

Flexilearn (UK)
http://www.flexiblelearning.co.uk
From the home page you can access links to education, training and management development. There are ready-to-use courses and resources for trainers. You can visit FlexiCareer Services, FlexiFreelance Services and FlexiWrite Services.

Gower (UK)
http://www.gowertraining.co.uk/
Visit the Gower Training Centre and you can link to its learning resource centre and training shop. Based in Aldershot, Hampshire, Gower is one of the UK's best known publishes of professional, business and management books.

Interactive Employment Training (USA)
http://www.hrtrain.com/
From this site, you can link into online courses, videos, CD-roms and computer-based training on sexual harassment, discipline, and other topics. The site is run by two American employment lawyers.

Institute of Personnel and Development (UK)
http://www.ipd.co.uk
With 100,00 members, the IPD is the leading UK professional body in this field. It publishes a range of authoritative books and training resources dealing with people management.

Vocational training sites ....

Intercultural Press (USA)
http://www.interculturalpress.com/
Intercultural Press is a well-known publisher of books and materials in the field of intercultural relations, mainly intended for people taking up posts in foreign countries. You can link into training, education and business from the home page.

Journal of Vocational Education and Training (UK)
http://www.triangle.co.uk/vae/00.htm
This is an international quarterly journal covering the development of practice and theory in work-related education, by acting as a focal point for the study of all aspects of vocational and pre-vocational education throughout the world. Links from the home page take you to the journal and to the publisher.

Kogan Page (UK)
http://www.kogan-page.co.uk
From the home page of this independent London-based business publisher you can link into resources for training, business and management and personal development.

MBA Games (UK)
http://www.mbagames.com/
This is a site for interactive management training games on the web. Its games include a business strategy simulation, management adventures in team leadership, and a skills test from the Institute of Management.

Microsoft Press (USA)
http://mspress.microsoft.com/
You can visit this site for books and interactive learning tools to help you get the most out of Microsoft technology.

National Training Resources Limited (UK)
http://www.national-training.co.uk/
The home page on this site details Confederation of Group Training Schemes (you can become a member). You can visit the training information news service for employment, TECs, Europe, training and FE, resources, conferences, management development, news and contacts. You can access reports taken from current issues of *Training Information News Service*, a twice-monthly publication for companies and individuals interested in training and development news (you can subscribe). It also runs a work-based self-development programme for managers.

Nichol (UK)
http://www.nicholl.co.uk/index.htm
From the home page of this Huddersfield-based firm, you can access resources for science and technology education and training. You can link into products, events, teacher notes, contacts and order lines.

Rhode Island Tech Prep (USA)
http://www.ri.net/TechPrep/tpworld.htm
From the home page, you can link to some useful vocational training resources from Canada, Europe, Germany, Australia and the Asian Pacific, with teacher contacts, discussion groups, a quarterly magazine, techprep across the world and other links.

Richardson Company Training Media (USA)
http://www.rctm.com/
This site details more than 100 producers of video and audiotapes, CD-roms and books, articles and games. There is a search engine and previews of video clips online.

Sandstone (UK)
http://www.sandstone.co.uk/
Find out about the Liberation training package for soft skills and the Dropzone training package for sales and customer care. The company also provides a number of other training services.

Self Improvement Training Web Sites (USA)
http://www.selfgrowth.com/corporate.html
This page is part of a huge site relating to self-development. It provides direct hyperlinks to more than 300 (mainly American) training resources and articles.

Skills for Work (UK)
http://www.man.ac.uk/careers/SkillsForWork/
This site details a report by the University of Manchester and the UMIST Careers Service which looks into the skills developed by higher education and how they relate to skills required by graduate employers. The home page is split into an Executive Summary and Appendices. From a list of choices you can link into the text. There is an employer questionnaire.

TCM Internet Services (USA)
http://www.tcm.com/trdev/
The site opens with The Training and Development Community Center, a gateway to resources for the T&D and HR community. There are links to jobs, resources, books, chat pages, conferences, discussion groups, Usenet news groups and trade publications.

Training Journal (UK)
http://www.trainingjournal.co.uk/
The monthly *Training Journal* (from Fenman, see above) offers training professionals regular news, book reviews, feature articles and commentary from leading practitioners in the field of training and human resource development.

Training Media Association (USA)
http://www.trainingmedia.org/
This is the American equivalent of the Training Media Copyright Associa-

tion in the UK. It includes in its membership almost every producer of training videos and multimedia within the USA.

Training Pages (UK)

http://www.trainingpages.co.uk/

Fig. 28. The Training Registry is an online directory for anything and everything to do with training. The data is continuously updated.

Training Pages provides information on professional training products and services, and a directory of professional business and management and IT training courses in the UK. You can search by listing or keyword. Training providers and freelance trainers are invited to add their own details.

Bookmarks   Location: http://www.trainingpages.co.uk/   ▼   Wha

TRAINING PAGES
training pages

Welcome to TrainingPages - the UK's premier *free* source of information for professional training products and services. You can search our classified listing or by keyword using the links below. Training providers (and soon) freelance trainers - just click here to add your details.

Training Pages is hiring. We have jobs for software developers and sales staff. Click here if you're interested.

Click a Category   Search Training Pages   About Training Pages

 Business and Management

 Information Technology

View Category Map

Search course details by keyword(s) *(multiple words must all be present to match)*. Use quotes "like this" to pick a phrase :

`internet skills`

- About Training Pages
- Additional Paid-For Services
- How to use Training Pages
- How can I be listed?
- Can I link to Training Pages?

Training Registry (USA)

http://www.tregistry.com/homefrme.htm

This is a directory of training courses, training providers, training products and services, training facilities, consulting services, professional speakers, and books.

Training Super Site (USA)

http://www.trainingsupersite.com/

The site brings together a range of resources including: publications, software downloads, a job bank, a learning centre, various directories, research, and chat rooms.

Training Zone (UK)

http://www.trainingzone.co.uk/

Training Zone is an everyday information service for professionals engaged in staff and organisational learning and development. It integrates a wide collection of resources, news, directories, events, reference material and databases. You can access online events, products and human resources. There are links, a search facility, latest postings and discussion forums. '8,500 organisations are networked through the UK's most popular site for training and HR professionals. Come and join them.'

UK-HRD (UK)
http://www.ukhrd.com/ukhrd/homeukhr.html
This is an email discussion forum for trainers and human resource specialists. The service is run by *Training Journal* and free to join.

Video Arts (UK)
http://www.videoarts.co.uk/
Video Arts was established in 1972 by a small group of television professionals, including John Cleese. Since then the company has become the world's leading provider of video-based multimedia learning programmes. Some 200 of its titles are in daily use by around 100,000 organisations worldwide. The programmes help train people in 50 countries.

VideoMedia (USA)
http://www.videomedia.net/
This site offers training solutions for business. You will find around 3,000 video previews and an online training catalogue.

Web-Based Training Cookbook (USA)
http://www.multimediatraining.com/cookbook.html
This 482-page book gives corporate trainers and business managers a recipe for effective use of the web to train employees and improve their performance. By focusing on the best methods of designing and creating web-training content, it explains how to learn from companies who are benefiting from using the web to supplement traditional training methods. Authoring tools, off-the-shelf courseware, and setting up a network for internet delivery are all explained. You will also receive a CD-rom featuring sample code for each type of web training page illustrated in the Cookbook, demos of web-based training programs, plus hotlinks to other web training sites, products and companies; the companion web site includes up-to-date information on web-based training and development topics. Naturally you can order the book.

Technology

Cyber Learning Centre (USA)
http://www.usa2100.org/
Here you can browse through a catalogue of over 200 computer-based training (CBT) products in the latest IT areas. The site is a project of the National Education Foundation and Northern Virginia Community College.

Women's Network for Technical and Vocational Education and Training (Australia)
http://sunsite.anu.edu.au/wnet/
This site represents a network of women in technical and vocational

education and training (TVET) in Australia and the Asia Pacific region. It enables women to access current TVET information and to discuss issues, ideas and achievements of women in the TVET sector. There are links to registration, bulletin boards, discussion groups, resources, newsletters and contacts.

Management training and development

Management Training and Development Institute (USA)
http://www.mtdi.com/
MTDI is a training, consulting, and research group. It helps organisations to improve their quality, productivity, and creativity by applying management theory and practice. It offers training, consulting, assessment, and research services to businesses and government agencies in the USA and elsewhere. It also conducts development programmes that support public and private sector technology-transfer initiatives worldwide.

Third Sector Project (USA)
http://www.jhu.edu/~ips/Programs/ThirdSectorProject/our.htm
Underlying the Hopkins Third Sector Project work is a concept that gears the training of non-profit managers to the philosophy of the non-profit sector, combining professional managerial capability with a serious commitment to empowerment of organisations, communities, and individuals through enablement training and management training. This is delivered through short-term internships, training workshops and training-the-trainer programs.

Thunderbird (USA)
http://www.t-bird.edu/
This is a project of the American Graduate School of International Management. There are links to executive education, overseas programs, library, commercial services, career management, research, site map, and feedback. Additional icons will take you to Campus Intranet and Alumni Intranet.

Vocational education and training around the world

Canadian Vocational Association (Canada)
http://www.cva.ca/
The site for this group links to its electronic discussion group, its quarterly magazine and a list of contacts at the group.

Electronic Training Village (Europe)
http://www.trainingvillage.gr/villagentry.asp
This site is originated by the European Centre for the Development of Vocational Training (CEDEFOP) and brings experts in the field of vocational training together. Material can be translated into German, French and English. Chats and conferences are held in a variety of languages, but predominantly English. Enter the site from Visitor's Info. From there you go to news, publication download, listserver row, opinions, registration, network and discussion groups.

European Centre for the Development of Vocational Training (Europe)
http://www.cedefop.gr/
Since 1976 CEDEFOP has been involved in promoting and developing vocational training of young people, and the continuing training of adults, primarily through European-wide co-ordination of analysis and research activities. There are links to study visits, publications, The Electronic Training Village, events and contacts.

Fig. 29. The Electronic Training Village is a valuable resource for vocational education and training within the countries of the European Union.

European Training Foundation (Europe)
http://www.etf.it/
This site is intended to help countries of central and eastern Europe and Central Asia learn from each other's vocational education and job training efforts. It provides the group's fact sheet, challenges and achievements, and recent reports, such as one highlighting vocational education efforts in the former Yugoslav Republic of Macedonia. It also lists contacts in member countries, including phone numbers, mailing addresses and, where applicable, email addresses.

Federal Institute for Vocational Training (Germany)
http://www.bibb.de/info96uk.htm
This site outlines Germany's vocational educational system, and details its budget and activities. It also provides contacts for its vocational educational offices, which manage curriculum, implementation and distance learning.

General and Vocational Education and Training (Germany)
http://www.uni-duisberg.de/FB2/BERU/publikat/young/inhalt/htm
This is a simple web site detailing the federal education system in Germany. It explains access to higher education, the central element of

vocational training and education in Germany, and the problems concerning the change in structure of the employment system and reasons for radical modernisation according to the new prototypical autonomously skilled worker as a model for the future.

LIFE (Germany)
http://www.oneworldweb.de/FrauenUmweltNetz/equal.e.htm
This site represents a joint group of European projects that have come together for the duration of a LEONARDO pilot project. The members are women educational providers from four countries of the EU who want to contribute to the better incorporation of ecology and equal opportunities for women and men into European vocational education. At the end of the project period (1998) ecological and ecotechnological qualification modules for electrical installation and plumbing were made available to specialists in the form of teaching materials, slide packages, videos and CD-roms.

National Centre for Vocational Education Research (Australia)
http://www.ncver.edu.au/ncver.htm
This is Australia's national vocational training research and developmental organisation. It outlines the group's current projects, such as studying the vocational education and training needs of higher education graduates, the needs of small companies and how vocational education can improve information technology. This site also contains the online version of the group's training magazine, a vocational education database and a list of upcoming conferences.

University of Western Australia (Australia)
http://www.library.uwa.edu.au/Resources/subjectpages/curresvoced.html
This site offers descriptions of and links to Australian curriculum resources in vocational education.

Vocational Education in G7 countries
http://nces.ed.gov/pubs/edvocg-7.html
This downloadable report describes and contrasts vocational education systems in the G7 countries (Canada, France, Germany, Japan, Italy, the United Kingdom, and the United States). In addition, the report describes some key cross-national indicators of the status of vocational education and compares data across countries. The report, about 450kb in length, is formatted in MS Word 6.0.

Vocational Education Web in Northern Europe (Europe)
http://www.abo.fi/vocweb/vw-en.htm
The main aim of the VocWeb project is to improve teaching and learning in vocational education colleges, to support computer network co-operation between schools and the use of the internet as an educational tool. It contains useful links for Denmark, Finland, Greenland, Iceland, Norway and Sweden.

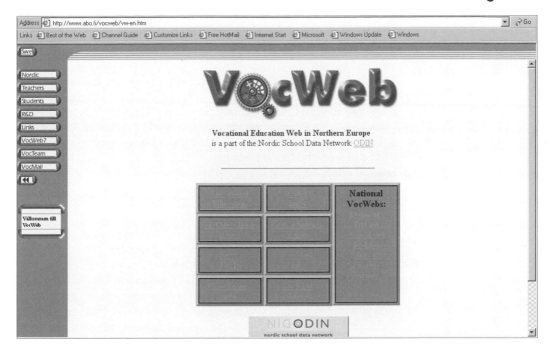

Vocational Training and Micro Credit (India)
http://www.aidindia.org/projects/vocational/aid.wm.html
A large part of the Indian population is unemployed or under-employed.
Housewives who want to supplement their family income with a produc-
tive vocation find it very difficult, either because they lack the skills or
because they lack the finance to make a start. Vocational training (and
following it up until the beneficiaries start earning), and making loans
easily accessible to the poor, are crucial for removing poverty and
under-employment. Recognising this, and realising that training women
helps the whole family, this project supports vocational training and micro
credit. Links offer insights into various projects.

Vocational Training Council (Hong Kong)
http://www.vtc.edu.hk/
The VTC has become the biggest vocational education organisation in
Hong Kong. It provides job-related training and education to more than
120,000 people every year through its Hong Kong Institute of Vocational
Education and 26 training centres. There are links to vocational education
and training, resources, conferences, news and contacts.

World Wide Vocational Education and Training
http://www.vtc.edu.hk/lib/net.voca.htm
This page contains links that provide information about vocational education and training. While preference is given to sites in Asia, the Pacific and
the USA, some useful sites of organisations in Europe are included.

Fig. 30. VocWeb, a site for
teachers and learners
seeking an overview of
vocational education in
northern Europe.

Qualifications awarding bodies

Assessment and Qualifications Alliance (UK)
http://www.aqa.org.uk
AQA is one of three unitary examining bodies in England. It was launched as a joint venture company in 1997 and registered as a charity a year later. It brought together the Associated Examining Board, the Northern Examinations and Assessment Board, and the City and Guilds' GNVQ qualification, which AQA acquired in 1998. AQA announced in October 1999 that AEB and NEAB had agreed to merge. AQA is now the biggest English unitary awarding body.

Associated Examining Board (UK)
http://www.aeb.org.uk
AEB provides public examinations, tests and related services for educational, training, industrial and commercial organisations. The home page provides an overview of AEB and on the left are click-on options. You can link into other sites such as City & Guilds. There is a link to AQA specifications. The coursework link gives general information about coursework and gives the opportunity to download documents. There is also a date and timetable section on the home page you can explore. There are loads of icons on the home page relating to the different courses. The 'support bag' offers contact links. The AEB and the NEAB have recently merged their identities into AQA.

Welcome to
City & Guilds

- City & Guilds
- City & Guilds International
- Nebs Management
- Pitman Qualifications
- Walled Garden

City & Guilds (UK)
http://www.city-and-guilds.co.uk
The left-hand side of the home page offers four options: City & Guilds background information, Pitman Qualifications, City & Guilds International and NEBS Management. From each of these sites you can explore further options. On the right-hand side of the home page five icons take you to the Walled Garden (unavailable at the time of writing), feedback, search, links and legal notices. At the foot of the home page there are five icons: news and events, senior awards, list of subjects, contacts, and FAQs.

Edexcel (UK)
http://www.edexcel.org.uk/
Edexcel is an international examining and awarding body. It provides a range of qualifications including GCSEs, GCE AS and A levels, GNVQs, BTEC First, National and Higher Certificates and Diplomas, NVQs, Key Skills and Entry Qualifications and specific programmes for employers. From the home page you can go to the introduction section that includes information about Edexcel such as background, key facts, people and departments and partnerships. Other options take you to information for centres, electronic publications (new users must register first) and site information. A useful site map and contact details are accessible from the home page.

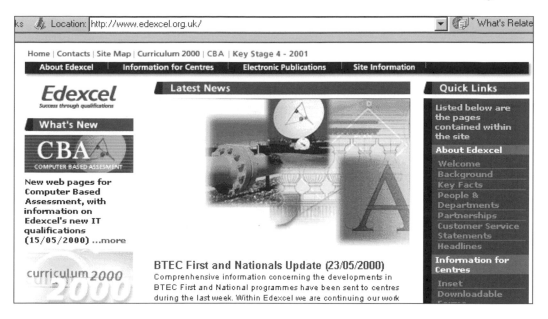

General National Vocational Qualifications (UK)
http://www.open.gov.uk/dfee/gnvq/gnvq.htm
GNVQs are an alternative to GCSE/GCE qualifications and job specific
National Vocational Qualifications (NVQs). They are mainly taken by 16 to
19 year-old students in full-time education. This DfEE site tells you what
GNVQs are, what GNVQs are available, what the entry requirements are,
where GNVQs can lead, GNVQs in the future, and other information including contact points.

Fig. 31. Edexcel is a
leading UK qualifications
awarding body. From its
home page you can
access centre information,
details of its electronic
publications, and the latest
newsflash.

London Chamber of Commerce and Industry Examinations Board (UK)
http://www.lccieb.org.uk/
The LCCIEB is a major international provider of vocational qualifications
and one of the UK's largest awarding bodies for National Vocational
Qualifications. All LCCIEB vocational qualifications are business-related
and have employer credibility. At the foot of the home page are icons
which link to LCCIEB qualifications, NVQs, publications, contact points,
news and regional representatives.

National Vocational Qualifications (UK)
http://www.lancs.ac.uk/users/cetad/nvqtext.htm
This is part of a larger web site belonging to the Centre for Training and
Development (CETAD) at Lancaster University. There is just one page on
this site providing an overview of NVQs, including benefits of NVQs to
companies and individuals, how NVQs work, how to achieve an NVQ and
features of the system. The page has a couple of click-on buttons leading
to more about NVQs offered by CETAD.

Northern Examinations and Assessment Board (UK)
http://www.neab.ac.uk/
The NEAB is a national provider of GCSE and GCE Advanced and AS

(Advanced Supplementary) examinations. It is also conducting pilot examinations in a new Certificate of Extended Studies, an exam between GCSE and GCE Advanced. The AEB and the NEAB have recently merged into AQA. Your can explore news and services and search for syllabuses.

OCR (UK)
http://www.ocr.org.uk
UCLES and the RSA Examinations Board have launched a new examining body, OCR (short for Oxford, Cambridge & RSA). It is designed to support the work of teachers and lecturers and to provide the best qualifications for their students. The home page has links to the background of OCR, a newsdesk, examination officer support, qualifications and a search facility. The newsdesk takes you into a choice of three or four other links. The qualification button gives access to information about GCSEs, AS and A levels, key skills, GNVQs and vocational qualifications.

Qualifications and Curriculum Authority (UK)
http://www.qca.org.uk/
The London-based QCA brings together the work of the National Council for Vocational Qualifications (NCVQ) and the School Curriculum and Assessment Authority (SCAA) with additional powers and duties. This gives it a unique overview of curriculum, assessment and qualifications across the whole of education and training. You can link to news, qualifications, education, lifelong learning, publications, and use the search function.

Fig 32. Qualifications for Industry (QFI) is recognised as one of the leading awarding bodies in the United Kingdom. Its portfolio of qualifications is constantly expanding.

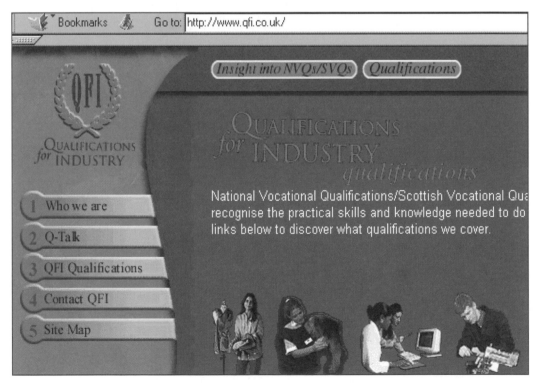

Qualifications for Industry (UK)
http://www.qfi.co.uk
QFI is the awarding body chosen by many of Britain's leading organisations. There are five icons on the home page. One tells you about QFI.
Another leads to Q-Talk, the electronic information service from QFI
which includes links to articles, other links and Q&A. The third takes you
into QFI industry qualifications. There is a contact icon and a link to a site
map and search facility.

Scottish Qualifications Authority (UK)
http://www.sqa.org.uk
The site details the qualifications which can be obtained through primary
and secondary schools, colleges, places of work and other training providers. It also features searchable databases of NC modules and HE units
as well as a separate section on SVQs. There are several options on the
left-hand side of the home page: a qualifications index and search faclity,
international work, a news desk, links, progressions routes, publications,
a bulletin board, contact points and a site map.

University of Cambridge Local Examinations Syndicate (UK)
http://www.ucles.org.uk
There are four main inks on the UCLES home page. One leads you to the
Cambridge International Examination home page which offers a very
clear site map. Another will take you to the OCR home page (http://
www.ocr.org.uk). The Cambridge EFL button brings up the home page
of the University of Cambridge Local Examination Syndicate, English as a
Foreign Language division. Finally there is an index and search button on
the home page.

Online vocational courses

4Training.com (USA)
http://www.4training.com/
This site offers links to various training opportunities such as computer
training, safety training, corporate training, vocational training, information and resources. There are also links to related sites including
4Universities and 4Colleges.

Aztec Software Associates (USA)
http://www.tregistry.com/aztec/
This site offers computer-based solutions to adult learning needs. All of
the modules in the Aztec Learning System combine to offer a wide variety
of lessons and adult education materials specifically designed to enhance
an employee's workplace skills. The competency-based courseware
deals with reading, writing, mathematics, business writing, clerical skills,
mechanical concepts, spatial relations, spelling, vocabulary and grammar.

Big Tree (Australia)
http://www.bigtree.com.au/
BigTree offers an integrated and interactive online learning environment. It

offers to help training providers discover new learning and training methods, expand prospective markets, and automate training administration. Big Tree can publish and host your training program. Authors and tutors can earn money as tutors and share expertise. Students can design their own learning programmes, choose from tutorials and courses, and communicate with fellow students overseas.

Fastrak Consulting (UK)
http://www.fastrak-consulting.co.uk/
This UK-based consultancy specialises in the application of technology to training and employee communications. From the home page you can go to features (e.g. how to evaluate online learning), an online trainer's toolkit, web-based training, links to related web sites (such as intranets), consultancy services, and contact points.

JER Group (USA)
http://www.jergroup.com/
JER offers accredited online workshops and tutorials courses for the internet learner: small business internet workshops, technical writing, creative writing, and digital graphics.

Home Education Network (USA)
http://www.OnlineLearning.net/Splash/
THEN offers distance learning on-line education through internet courses in business management, organisational behaviour, risk management, accounting, screenwriting, fiction writing, test preparation and teacher certification. Its online courseware is offered in conjunction with the UCLA Extension University. At-home study courses can be completed online or through employers and an affiliated intranet training and distance education network.

KnowledgePool

Search our site

vocational

Go

Links:

Enter
Online Training

Knowledge Pool Online
http://eu.knowledgepool.com/
With over 800 courses to choose from, Knowledge Pool claims to be the world's largest non-proprietary training organisation, offering computer software and project design and management training over the internet. Its distance learning material is supported 24 hours a day by online tutors through virtual classrooms. KnowledgePool comprises the training businesses of Fujitsu and ICL.

Online Education (UK)
http://www.online.edu/
Online Education Ltd (OLE) assists the development of working professionals by providing high recognised degree courses, such as MBA Management Practice, delivered within a framework of student support and service.

Online Learning (USA)
http://www.onlinelearning.net/
Online Learning is a California-based supplier of continuing higher educa-

tion. You can choose from a wide variety of certificated and sequential online programs and courses designed with your career in mind. Visit the 'available classes' page for more details.

Online Resources (Australia)
http://www.tdd.nsw.edu.au/tdd/resources/
This is a page of the Training and Development Directorate, part of the New South Wales Department of Education and Training. It supports NSW public schools by providing training for teachers and staff. You can link into learning programs, publications, newsletters, research conferences and retraining opportunities.

University of Phoenix (USA)
http://www.uophx.edu
This site offers graduate and undergraduate degree programs to working professionals around the world. With 51 campuses and learning centres located throughout the US and the Commonwealth of Puerto Rico, including the Online Degree Program and Centre for Distance Education, the University of Phoenix is one of the largest private accredited institutions for business and management in the United States.

Vocational training links

American Society for Training and Development (USA)
http://www.astd.org/
This is a site for workplace learning and development. You can access links to the market place (jobs, conferences and books), a library facility

Fig. 33. UK Training Access Points. The site allows you to choose the level of study, the method of learning and the course provider; it also lists subject areas.

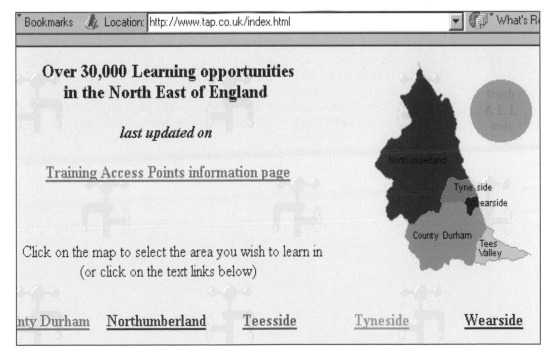

81

and 'communities of practice' (different subject areas), products and services, forums, research and policies.

Training Access Points (UK)
http://www.tap.co.uk/index.html
Click on the map on the home page to access over 30,000 learning opportunities in the north east of England.

Training and Enterprise Councils (UK)
http://www.tec.co.uk/
This site offers quick links to all the local TEC offices across the UK, a few of which have their own web pages.

Training Resources (UK)
http://www.geocities.com/Athens/Acropolis/3982/training.html
This site presents links to a number of key training and development sites including UK Training Pages, Centre for Workforce Development and ASTD Training Marketplace among others.

Training for business owners

Virtual Business University (USA)
http://www.virtualbusinessu.com/
VBU is a virtual training provider based in West Virginia, dedicated to teaching business owners how to use the internet as a business tool. Sample 'teleclasses' include: Increase traffic to your web site, Start your own email newsletter broadcast, and Develop your own business: a virtual assistant.

Virtual University for Small and Medium Sized Enterprises (USA)
http://www.vusme.com/
VUSME uses courses and case studies to help entrepreneurs use the internet to develop profitable businesses. It makes its courses available through organisations that support and service the small business community: colleges and universities, business and professional associations, training and development institutions, consultants and banks.

Research centres and government offices

British Training International (UK)
http://www.bti.org.uk/
This is an official government site set up to represent its partner organisations and the UK government in promoting vocational excellence internationally. Its aim is to promote the UK as a world leader in developing vocational systems of education, training and related services.

Department for Education and Employment (DfEE)
http://www.dfee.gov.uk/
There is a search facility on the home page of this official site where you can find documents relating to a particular topic. The site index states

Fig. 34. The UK Department for Education and Employment.

what's new, for example the 'New Deal' for schools. By clicking onto an alphabetical letter, you can view a list of topics beginning with that letter e.g. 'Individual Learning Accounts' was one of ten under the letter I. You can view DfEE circulars and publications, get summaries and downloads. Under Publication, a list of topic areas is shown, from which you can view individual publications. The links option brings up related sites such as the Teacher Training Agency. The News link offers recent DfEE press releases.

European Social Fund (Europe)
http://www.esf.ie/
ESF promotes employment and develop human resources throughout Europe. Its aim is to help people find, keep, or regain work.

Industrial and Vocational Training Board (USA)
http://ncb.intnct.mu/ivtb.htm
The IVTB functions under the Ministry of Environment, Human Resource Development and Employment. It exists to plan, monitor and evaluate training programmes to design and develop training curricula, to imple ment training schemes and training programmes and to finance the training of school leavers and employees through a levy/grant system. There are corporate links, training initiatives, courses, centres registration, resources and contacts.

International Society for Performance Improvement (USA)
http://www.ispi.org/
ISPI is an international association dedicated to improving productivity

and performance in the workplace. It represents more than 10,000 members throughout the United States, Canada and 40 other countries. From the home page you can find out about ISPI, what's new, professional services (jobs, conferences), publications and membership. There is a search facility.

National Center for Research in Vocational Education (USA)
http://ncrve.berkeley.edu/MDS-1205/
NCRVE is based at University of California and is engaged in research, development, dissemination and outreach in work-related education. It mission is to strengthen school-based and work-based learning to prepare all individuals for lasting and rewarding employment, further education, and lifelong learning.

Office of Vocational Education and Training (Australia)
http://www.dvet.tas.gov.au/
Produced by the Tasmanian Department of Education this site offers links to the Tasmanian VET system, policy and funding, publications and resources, useful links, contacts and training and vocational information.

Research Centre for Vocational Education and Training (Australia)
http://www.rcvet.uts.edu.au/
RCVET (the University of Technology, Sydney) conducts research into vocational education and training (VET). It considers vocational learning and assessment, VET systems, and participation in VET and policy. It disseminates the findings of research to industry, government, training providers, other researchers and the public, provides strategic support to researchers and practitioners, strengthening research culture throughout the VET sector and informs, supports and influences policy in the VET sector. There are links to news, research, publication, useful links and contacts, and you can download papers.

Training Standards Council (UK)
http://www.tsc.gov.uk/
The TSC is responsible for the UK's national training inspectorate. Inspectors assess the quality of some 2,000 training providers, working throughout England, and report on each one every four years. You can access news and circulars, schedules, reports, contacts and links.

University for Industry (UK)
http://national.learning.net.uk/
The National Learning Network is a research network for the University for Industry, a new initiative of the British government. The site explains such topics as the need for a university for industry, learning on demand, how it would work, establishing priorities, stimulating activities, taking learning to the workplace, home and community, supporting and motivating the learner, and organisation and funding.

Related chapters

Chapter 5 – Occupational training web sites
Chapter 7 – Distance and online learning web sites
Chapter 8 – Specialist web sites for particular groups

Related Internet Handbooks

Careers Guidance on the Internet, Laurel Alexander (Internet Handbooks).

5 Occupational training sites

In this chapter we will explore:

▶ *future trends in occupational growth*
▶ *occupational training web sites*

. . . .

Future trends in occupational growth

When considering occupational training, we should keep in mind the occupations with a future. The long-term shift from goods-producing to service-producing employment is expected to continue. Service industries – transport, communications, and utilities; retail and wholesale trades; services; government; and finance, insurance, and property – are expected to grow. In addition, the services divisions within these sectors, which include health, business, and educational services, are set to expand.

Services are both the largest and the fastest growing division within the service sector. Work will be found in banking, hospitals, data processing, and management consulting. The two largest industry groups in this division – health services and business services – are projected to continue to grow very fast. Social, legal, and engineering and management services industries further illustrate this division's strong growth.

Fig. 35. Using the Yahoo! search engine to explore web sites dealing with occupational training.

Business services
Business services will generate many jobs. Personnel supply services, made up primarily of employment (especially temporary and interim staff) agencies, are the largest sector in this group and will continue to

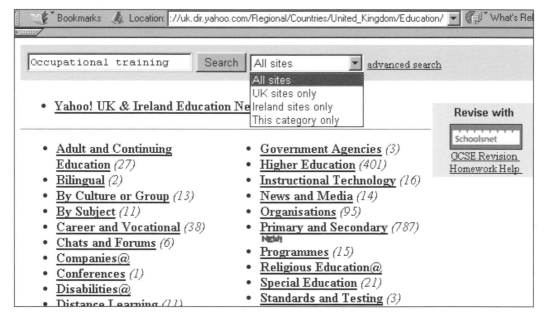

86

add many jobs. Business services also include one of the fastest growing industries in the economy – computer and data-processing services. This industry's rapid growth stems from advances in technology, worldwide trends toward office and factory automation, and increases in demand from business and individuals. Continued rising enrolments of older, foreign, and part-time students are expected to enhance employment in post-secondary education. Support workers, counsellors, and administrative staff within the education system is projected to increase. Employment in clerical occupations related to banking, finance and insurance has increased sharply as a result of developments such as telesales and the automation of administrative systems.

Health services
Health care will continue to be one of the fastest growing industries in the economy. Improvements in medical technology, and a growing and ageing population, will increase the demand for health services. Employment in home health care services – the fastest growing industry in the economy – nursing homes, and offices and clinics of health practitioners is projected to increase. For example, residential care institutions, which provide round-the-clock assistance to older persons and others who have limited ability for self-care, is projected to be one of the fastest growing industries. Other social services industries set for rapid growth include child day-care services and individual and miscellaneous social services, including elderly day care and family social services.

Retail services
Guided by higher levels of personal income and continued increases in women's labour force participation, the fastest projected job growth in retail trade is in apparel and accessory outlets and eating and drinking establishments, with the latter employing the most workers in this sector. Substantial numerical increases in retail employment are anticipated in food stores, car sales and general merchandise outlets.

Financial services
The demand for financial products and services is expected to continue unabated, but bank mergers, consolidations, and closings resulting from competition from non-bank corporations that offer bank-like services, are expected to limit job growth. The fastest growing industry within this sector is expected to be non-depository holding and investment offices, which includes businesses that compete with banks, such as finance companies and mortgage brokers.

Transport services
Road transportation will account for a high number of new jobs as will air transportation. The projected gains in transportation jobs reflect the continued shift from rail to road freight transportation, rising personal incomes, and growth in foreign trade. In addition, changes in the transportation industry have increased personal and business travel options, spurring strong job growth in the passenger transportation arrangement industry, which includes travel agencies.

Occupational training sites..

Construction

Construction, the only goods-producing industry is projected to grow. Increases in road and bridge construction will offset the slowdown in demand for new housing, reflecting the slowdown in population growth and the over-expansion of office building construction in recent years.

Manufacturing

The projected loss of manufacturing jobs reflects productivity gains achieved from increased investment in manufacturing technologies as well as a winnowing-out of less efficient operations. The composition of manufacturing employment is expected to shift since most of the jobs that will disappear are production jobs. The number of professional, technical, and managerial positions in manufacturing firms will increase.

Although service sector growth will generate millions of clerical, sales, and service jobs, it also will create jobs for financial managers, engineers, nurses, electrical and electronics technicians, and many other managerial, professional, and technical workers. In fact, the fastest growing occupations will be those that require the most formal education and training. Occupations and industries covered in this chapter include:

Accounting	Hairdressing and beauty	Print industry
Acupressure massage	Health & human services	Probation work
Banking		Property
Barrister	Heritage	Psychiatry
Care of exotic animals	Hospitality	Psychology
Cleaning	Hypnotherapy	Reflexology
Clothing	Industrial training	Sailing
Coaching	Insurance	Science
Community work	Investment analysis	Security industry
Computing	Information technology	
Conservation		Social services
Construction	Local government	Social work
Costumier	Management	Special needs management
Dental profession	Marine industry	
Design and technology	Massage	Sports and recreation
Diet and nutrition	Meat industry	Stage management
Electrical industry	Motor industry	Teacher training
Electronics	Nursing	Telecommunications
Engineering	Occupational therapy	Teleworking
Forensic science	Offshore oil	Travel industry
Fork list operation	Performing	Theatre management
Fund management	Pharmaceuticals	
Gas-related sectors	Policing	TV & media
Glass industry	Ports	Water industry

Occupational training web sites

Academy of Curative Hypnotherapists (UK)
http://www.ach.co.uk/
The ACH is a non-profit making organisation, established by qualified, experienced and practising hypnotherapists. You can link into their foundation course, diploma course, workshops, membership list and contact points.

Amazing Exotics Education Center (USA)
http://www.amazingexotics.com/
This is a sophisticated web site offering among other things, an educational area that provides training in management, husbandry, performance and the care of exotic animals.

Animal Care & Equine Training Organisation (UK)
http://www.horsecareers.co.uk/
Through this site you can find out about NVQs and SVQs, national traineeships, modern apprenticeships, an interactive catalogue of all the UK's courses and colleges, plus a bulletin board and further links.

Association for Psychological Therapics (UK)
http://www.apt.uk.com/
The APT posts details of training courses for professional carers – psychiatrists, psychologists, nurses, social workers, occupational therapists and teachers – covering a range of psychological therapy-related topics.

Baker College (USA)
http://www.baker.edu
The college offers some 75 diploma, certificate, associate, bachelor, and masters programs in business, health and human services, technical subjects, and engineering.

Board for Education and Training in the Water Industry (UK)
http://www.betwi.demon.co.uk/noframe.htm
BETWI was established in 1992 to act as the industry training organisation (ITO) and lead body for the UK water sector. As a national training organisation (NTO), BETWI is a government-recognised organisation and national strategist for the water sector. It has the key responsibility for developing education and training arrangements in the water sector. It has a primary role in galvanising employer involvement in the development and take-up of competence-based occupational standards, education, training and qualifications to improve sector competitiveness both at home and abroad.

BPP (UK)
http://www.bppluton.co.uk/
Through the site of this publicly-quoted professional training company, you can access fast track courses towards all the major accounting, business and legal qualifications in the UK.

Occupational training sites...

Bristol Old Vic Theatre School (UK)
http://oldvic.drama.ac.uk/
This is an industry-led vocational training establishment preparing actors, actresses, stage managers, carpenters, electricians, sound technicians, costumiers, designers, property makers and directors for careers in theatre, radio, television, film, trade presentations, recording studios and other areas of employment.

California College for Health Sciences (USA)
http://www.cchs.edu/
You can link into accredited distance-learning programs that offer working professionals the freedom to complete a college degree while continuing to meet other commitments.

Canterbury Christ Church University College (UK)
http://www.canterbury.ac.uk/depts/acad/ot/admission.htm
This is a page from the Department of Occupational Therapy, explaining admission requirements for its occupational therapy training course. People interested in qualifying as an occupational therapist need to apply through UCAS.

CAPITB Trust (UK)
http://www.careers-in-clothing.co.uk/
This is the national training organisation for the British clothing industry responsible for promoting careers, education, and vocational qualifications. You can find details here of their work, and seek help if you are considering a career in the industry.

Capitol College (USA)
http://www.capitol-college.edu
Capitol College is dedicated to education for advanced technology industries. It has developed Active Class, a web-based virtual learning environment. Its open content means that educators can use their existing electronic course materials, from Word documents and PowerPoint presentation slides to HTML, Java and audio/video files, without having to recreate them for a proprietary format.

Certify Now (UK)
http://www.certifynow.co.uk/
This is a one-stop resource for certification information. You can click onto the UK training centre list, newsletters, courses, trainer's resources, downloads, CBT and study books. This is a vast information resource for those seeking professional computing qualifications.

CISC (UK)
http://www.cisc.org.uk/
This is a forum for NVQs/SVQs at professional, managerial and technical levels in planning, construction, property and related engineering services. There are links to the national occupational standards database, a newsletter, contacts and forthcoming events.

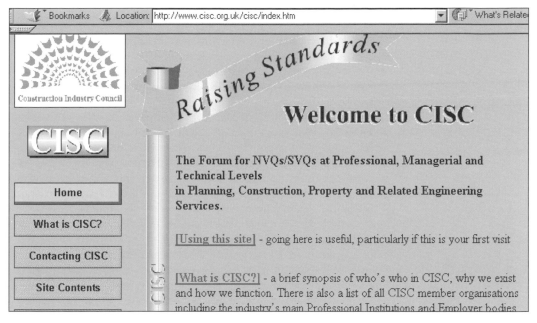

Fig. 36. The Construction Industry Standing Conference (CISC) was formed in 1990 to set standards of competence for professional, managerial and technical roles for all sectors of the construction industry.

CMEPlus (UK)
http://www.ukpractice.net/open/partners/cme.plus/index.htm
This is an educational service for family doctors that directs GPs to various medical and other courses, web resources and training schemes.

Committee on Vocational Training for England and Wales (UK)
http://www.eastman.ucl.ac.uk/cvt/index.html
The Committee – CVT for short – is representative of all branches of the dental profession. Its remit is to formulate guidance for, and monitor standards within, locally managed dental vocational training schemes for new entrants to GDP. You can use this web site to find out more about VT, how to become involved as trainer, VDP or adviser, how to download text for inclusion in trainer and VDP handbooks or other VT scheme literature.

Community Justice National Training Organisations (UK)
http://www.communityjusticento.co.uk/
London-based CJNTO promotes training and development for people in professions involved with crime prevention and working with offenders and victims of crime, such as police, probation staff, community volunteers and council workers.

Community Work Resources (UK)
http://www.community-work-training.org.uk/
The site is produced by the West Yorkshire Community Work Training Group and offers training material for community workers and others working in community based settings, material on anti-discriminatory practice and links to other useful sites.

Occupational training sites...

Conference of Drama Schools (UK)
http://www.drama.ac.uk/
This site offers links to current CDS drama sites, spotlight casting UK, and to a few top drama schools in the UK.

Design and Technology Association (UK)
http://www.data.org.uk/
DATA is the recognised professional body representing people involved in design and technology education. It develops a high quality curriculum which engages young people in designing, enhancing the quality of teaching and learning in design and technology and working with industry and commerce to ensure that the benefits of such experiences permeate the curriculum at all levels. You can link into T & D, publications, resources, recruitment, conference information and contacts.

Distance Learning Centre (UK)
http://www.user.globalnet.co.uk/~dlc/index.htm
If you would like a British qualification which will help you gain entry into nurse training, university or initial teacher training, the DLC can offer you a kite-marked access course which is validated by the Open College Network. Studying with DLC means that you can work at home but still maintain a direct link to your own personal tutor either through the internet, by post, or by telephone.

Education International Worldwide (USA)
http://www.eiworldwide.com/
You can search the databases of business, engineering, and English language programs at universities and colleges in five countries (Australia, Canada, New Zealand, UK, and USA).

Inns of Court School of Law (UK)
http://www.icsl.ac.uk/
The school, in central London, offers a course of training for people who want to become barristers at law. There are 750 full-time and 100 part-time students, with 45 academic staff, helped by 110 practising barristers.

Institute of Investment Management and Research (UK)
http://www.iimr.org.uk/
The IIMR is the professional body which awards qualifications for the profession of investment analyst and fund manager. On the web site you can try the Exam Game – print out a specimen exam with examiner comments. The members' forum provides a space for members to discuss the latest investment issues. You can visit the library to read articles from its journal, the *Professional Investor*. There is also an events diary, and details of publication and training providers.

Institute of Management (UK)
http://www.inst-mgt.org.uk/
The mission of the Institute of Management is to promote the art and science of management. From this site you can access information

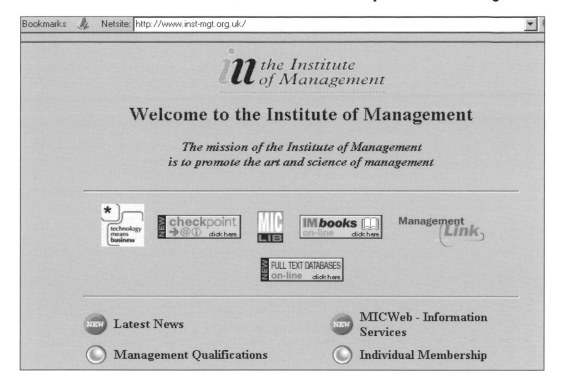

about management qualifications, membership, career development, and contacts.

International Therapy Examination Council (UK)
http://www.therapies.com/itec/itec.htm
This site offers qualifying courses in alternative therapies such as massage, anatomy and physiology, Indian head massage, reflexology, diet and nutrition, aromatherapy and acupressure massage. It also runs correspondence courses.

Lantra National Organisation Training (UK)
http://www.eto.co.uk/
Caring for the environment is central to Lantra's work. Its site is aimed at everyone interested in environmental conservation, skills, education, jobs, careers, work and training, including students, volunteers and employees, employers and training and education providers. You can click on to N/SVQs, national traineeships and modern apprenticeships. ETO in its web site address stands for Environmental Training Organisation.

Mentor MA (UK)
http://www.mentor.org.uk/
Here you will find information about vocational training courses and apprenticeships in beauty therapy, administration and hairdressing 'throughout Scotland as well as many other European countries' provided by this Edinburgh company.

Fig. 37. The Institute of Management invites both individual and corporate membership. There are lots of options on the home page including book ordering.

Occupational training sites...

Metier (UK)
http://www.metier.org.uk/
Metier is the UK's National Training Organisation (NTO) for half a million people working in the arts and entertainment industries. It provides career advice and information about the qualifications available for aspiring performers, and for those who want to work behind the scenes. The site includes details of standards and qualifications, and educational support materials.

Modern Apprenticeship for the Construction Industry (UK)
http://www.sheffieldtec.co.uk/wbdp/masum/construc.htm
The site contains a summary of the Modern Apprenticeship Framework.

Motor Industry Training Council (UK)
http://www.mitc.co.uk/
This is the organisation responsible for education and training in the UK motor trade. Its site contains details of courses and qualifications for those involved in the repair, maintenance and supply of vehicles and parts.

National Coaching Foundation (UK)
http://www.ncf.org.uk/
The NCF works to improve the quality of coaching in sport in the United Kingdom by enabling the education and continuous development of coaches at all levels. Through this site, you can link into education and information, products and courses, contacts, membership details, and a bulletin board.

National Council of Further Education (UK)
http://www.ncfe.org.uk/
The NCFE offers a wide range of high quality outcomes-based vocationally-related qualifications designed to meet the education and training needs of employers, employees and individuals. NCFE qualifications are offered by more than 500 further education sector colleges, adult education centres, training providers, schools and businesses.

National Examining Board for Supervisory Management (UK)
http://www.nebsmgt.co.uk/
Linked with City & Guilds, NEBS Management offers a comprehensive range of nationally and internationally recognised qualifications to meet the needs of today's managers at all levels across industry. Through its site you can access information about management training and development courses and workshops at more than 1,000 centres across the UK and Ireland.

National Occupational Standards (UK)
http://www.doh.gov.uk/swro/0405.htm
Through this official Department of Health site, you will find some links to occupational standards within the NHS and Health Education Authority.

National Occupational Standards

Other relevant links in this web site :

Distribution of Work

Education & Training Developments

Interprofessional Education and Training

 The Strategic Use of Occupational
Standards in the NHS

Health Education Authority
Professional Development

National Online Training Centre (USA)
http://www.nnlm.nlm.nih.gov/mar/online/index.html
Here you can access training information from the National Library of
Medicine databases, and explore databanks with links taking you to training schedules, class descriptions, registrations, contacts, publications
and self-instructional resources.

Netform (UK)
http://www.netform.co.uk/
Netform is a European network for managing organisational change and
improving the quality of managers in vocational education and training. It
is a project supported by the Leonardo da Vinci Programme of the Commission of the European Communities.

Promoting Science, Engineering and Technology (UK)
http://www.set4women.gov.uk/set4women/return/index.htm
The SET for Women Unit was created following a recommendation in the
1994 *Rising Tide* report. It exists to support women in developing fulfilling
and rewarding careers in higher education, industry and teaching. Various
links lead you to material and other sites dealing with key issues such as
networking, careers, family-friendly policies, research, role models, returning to work, and funding schemes.

Prospects (UK)
http://www.btinternet.com/ ~ prospects.training/occupati.htm
Prospects provides training services spanning a wide range of occupational areas such as IT, engineering, construction, health and safety and
management.

Fig. 38. National
Occupational Standards
for health workers.

Occupational training sites. . . . .

Sail Sussex (UK)
http://www.sailsussex.freeserve.co.uk/
Here you will find a range of training courses and qualifications (RYA approved) in dinghy sailing, power boating and personal watercraft.

Security Industry Training Organisation (UK)
http://www.sito.co.uk/
SITO is a leading UK provider of qualifications for the security industry. You can link into news, conferences, standards, training, qualifications, projects and further links.

SETNET (UK)
http://www.setnet.org.uk/pages/set0i4.htm
This is a site for the Science Engineering Technology Mathematics Network. It is a joint venture of 30 information points which informs UK teachers, business and industry about science, engineering, technology and maths-related schemes and initiatives nationwide.

STS Training (UK)
http://www.sts-training.co.uk/
STS offers a wide range of training programmes, including national traineeships, modern apprenticeships, special needs training, New Deal, work-based training for adults and skills for small businesses.

Telelink Training for Europe (UK)
http://www.marble.ac.uk/telep/telework/tlpfolder/tlp.html
This is a European Community Euroform-funded project to develop training opportunities in the field of teleworking and has already defined a Level II, Restricted Vocational Qualification (RVQ) for teleworkers. It has established a growing network of TeleLink Centres (TeleCottages and Training Centres) around Europe which can provide training support and service points for telework skills. The TeleLink project has also developed a Level III National Vocational Qualification (NVQ) for teleworker supervisors and is currently defining a Level IV Vocational Qualification for telecottage managers.

Total Active Care & Communication Training (UK)
http://www.rhymer.demon.co.uk/
This training company specialises in teaching programmes for UK care professionals, offering NVQs in care, special needs housing, and management.

Transport Training Services (UK)
http://bquest.newsquestmidlands.co.uk/tts/
TTS delivers in-house forklift operator training. In-house training gives new or already qualified drivers the advantage of being trained and gaining firsthand and sometimes unique experience of their own working conditions and environment.

Travel Training Company (UK)
http://www.tttc.co.uk/
The Travel Training Company is the main UK provider of training and qualifications for people seeking a career in travel or already working within the travel industry. Based in Woking, Surrey, it is a wholly owned commercial subsidiary of the Association of British Travel Agents (ABTA).

UK College
http://www.ukcollege.com/
This private college specialises in training healthcare professionals in hypnotherapy and complementary medicine. It offers City & Guilds and BTEC certificates.

Videotel Marine International (UK)
http://www.videotel.co.uk/
From the home page, you can link into video and computer training packages for the marine industry, offshore oil and gas-related sectors and safety packages for other selected industries.

Virtual College (UK)
http://www.virtual-college.co.uk
This site offers multimedia-based training for the electronics manufacturing industry.

Warrington Collegiate Institute (UK)
http://www.warr.ac.uk/
Anyone keen to get into the television business should look here: the institute offers MA courses in television, media and screen studies, and has a tie-in with Manchester-based Granada TV.

A selection of UK National Training Organisations (NTOs)

British Ports Industry Training
http://bpit.co.uk

Banking and Building Societies National Training Organisation (UK)
http://www.bbsnto.org

Cleaning and Support Services National Training Organisation (UK)
http://www.cleaningnto.org

Cultural Heritage NTO (UK)
http://www.chnto.co.uk

Electricity Training Association (UK)
http://www.eta.org.uk

Electronics and Software Services NTO (UK)
http://www.ess.org.uk

Occupational training sites..

Fig. 39. The web site of
the Electricity Training
Organisation (ETA), the
recognised national
training organisation for
the electricity industry. It is
responsible for developing
technical standards of
competence and National
and Scottish Vocational
Qualifications.

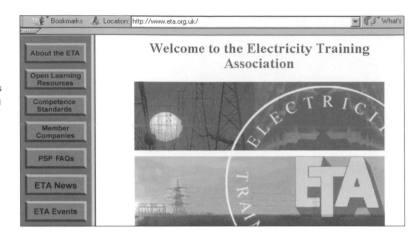

Engineering and Marine Training Authority (UK)
http://www.emta.org.uk

Engineering Construction ITB (UK)
http://www.ecitb.org.uk

Food and Drink NTO (UK)
http://www.foodandrinknto.org.uk

Gas Industry NTO (UK)
http://www.ginto.co.uk

Glass Training Limited (UK)
http://www.glasstrg.demon.co.uk

Hairdressing and Beauty Industry Authority (UK)
http://www.habia.org.uk

Hospitality Training Foundation (UK)
http://www.htf.org.uk

Insurance and Related Financial Services NTO (UK)
http://www.cii.co.uk/nto.htm

Local Government NTO (UK)
http://www.lgmb.gov.uk

Management and Enterprise NTO (UK)
http://www.meto.org.uk

Meat Training Council (UK)
http://www.meattraining.org.uk

Motor Industry Training Council (UK)
http://www.mitc.co.uk

Pharmaceutical Industry NTO (UK)
http://www.abpi.org.uk

Print and Graphic Communication NTO (UK)
http://www.bpif.org.uk

Science, Technology and Mathematics Council (UK)
http://www.stmc.org.uk/

Sports and Recreation NTO (UK)
http://www.sprito.org.uk

Telecommunications Vocational Standards Council (UK)
http://www.tvsc-nto.org.uk

Training Organisation for Personal Social Services (UK)
http://www.topss.org.uk

Fig. 40. SPRITO is the national UK training organisation for sport, recreation, and allied occupations. You can easily search here for approved centres offering access to the relevant S/NVQs.

Related chapters

Chapter 3 – University web sites
Chapter 4 – Vocational training web sites
Chapter 7 – Distance and online learning web sites
Chapter 9 – Best of the rest

Related Internet Handbooks

Careers Guidance on the Internet, Laurel Alexander (Internet Hand-
    books).
Finding a Job on the Internet, Brendan Murphy (Internet Handbooks).

6 Adult education sites

In this chapter we will explore:

▶ *adult education links*
▶ *online and distance adult learning providers*
▶ *special interest courses*
▶ *learning guidance providers*

Introduction

'The national Learning and Skills Council will have two committees one for young people's learning, the other for adult learning. The Adult Learning Committee will be responsible for advising the Council on achieving the National Learning Targets for adults and for organisations, on raising and widening participation and for advising on:

Fig. 41. The National Institute of Adult Continuing Education (NIACE). It has a particular concern for widening access to learning opportunities and increasing participation among groups under-represented in education and training.

1. adult education and training in further education colleges
2. adult learning at home and in the community
3. workforce development including the promotion of NVQs and Investors in People
4. more flexible access to learning
5. information, advice and guidance for adults'

(Source: *NIACE briefing on the Government White Paper*, 1999).

Adults face their own challenges in learning, as there are challenges with every age. With reference to adults however, there are often issues around literacy and numeracy and learning difficulties. Other groups which tend to be under-represented in education and training include older adults, refugees and some minority ethnic communities, many men, some groups of women, unemployed people, those without qualifications and unskilled manual workers.

In essence, adult education crosses over several of the chapters in this book. However, the focus for this chapter is specifically on sites which state that they specialise in adult learners. Much of the learning is leisure- or self-development based, but there are several sites offering accredited or qualification level courses.

Adult education links

Adult Residential Colleges Association (UK)
http://www.aredu.demon.co.uk/
The ARCA colleges are a group of small colleges specialising in short-stay residential adult education courses for the general public. Many are run by local authorities, while others are operated by charitable trusts or similar organisations. Through this site you can access study tours abroad, courses, links, becoming a member and meeting other students.

Age Concern (UK)
http://www.ace.org.uk
Age Concern undertakes to promote the development of education opportunities for older people. You can visit its education bulletin and other publications.

American Association for Adult and Continuing Education (USA)
http://www.albany.edu/aaace/
AAACE is the nation's premier organisation dedicated to adult learning. With members from 60 affiliates and 40 nations, it represents its members from secondary and post-secondary education, business and labour, military and government and from community-based organisations. It publishes three of the nation's leading periodicals in education and training: *Adult Learning* magazine, the scholarly journal *Adult Education Quarterly* and the journal *Adult Basic Education*. It also publishes books, monographs and booklets on a variety of adult education topics. You can use this site to access bulletin boards, conferences and other links.

Basic Skills Agency (UK)
http://www.basic-skills.co.uk
This is the national development agency for literacy, numeracy and related basic skills across England and Wales. You can link to consultancy services, funding, learning material, conferences and leaflets. A freephone service (0800 700 987) offers to help adults with their basic skills.

Caribbean Regional Council for Adult Education (West Indies)
http://www.internet-club.com/trinidad-and-tobago/carcae/
CARCAE was set up as an umbrella organisation for adult education in the

Dutch, English, French and Papiamento-speaking Caribbean. There are links to the 19 institutional and individual member territories as well as access to the regional agenda for adult education and the Sixth General Assembly.

Commonwealth Open University (West Indies)
http://www.geocities.com/CollegePark/5703/
The Commonwealth Open University Ltd is an international institution registered and established in the British Virgin Islands. It provides adult continuing education and was developed to meet the needs of adults by offering non-resident degree and other programs on an international basis.

Community Matters (UK)
http://www.communitymatters.org.uk
Community Matters is a nationwide federation of community associations and similar organisations, with around 850 member organisations in England, Wales and Scotland. It brings together community education and other neighbourhood groups concerned with the well-being of their community and its social, recreational and adult education needs.

Cornwall Adult Education (UK)
http://business.thisiscornwall.co.uk/adult-education/
You can link into this guide to adult education in Cornwall and access the venues and courses on offer.

Elderhostel Adult Education (USA)
http://www.elderhostel.org/
Elderhostel Inc is a not-for-profit organisation with 25 years' experience of providing educational adventures for adults aged 55 and above. These short-term educational programs offer a stimulating way to share new ideas, explore new places and make new friends.

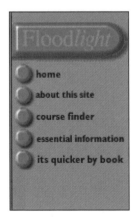

Floodlight (UK)
http://www.floodlight.co.uk/
Through the home page on this site, you can access this established and official guide to full-time and part-time courses all over London.

National Federation of Women's Institutes (UK)
http://www.nfwi.org.uk
The NFWI is a non-party political, non-sectarian voluntary organisation that provides democratically controlled educational opportunities for country-minded women.

National Institute of Adult Continuing Education (UK)
http://www.niace.org.uk/
Leicester-based NIACE is a leading pubic organisation for adult learning in England and Wales. Its work crosses the boundaries of post-school education and training. It works in all fields of UK education and training, including local authority provision, the further education college sector,

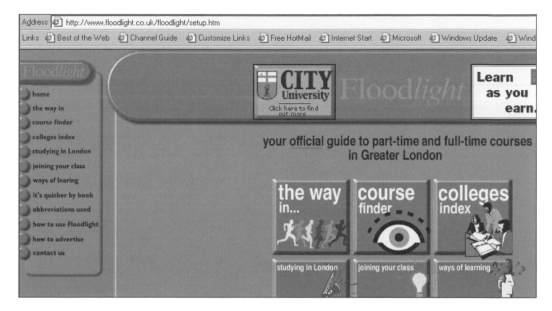

Fig. 42. *Floodlight* is an established guide to part-time and full-time courses in Greater London. Use the search function on its web site to find the training opportunities you want.

higher education in universities and colleges of HE, employment-led learning involving both employers and trade unions, learning in the voluntary sector, and learning through the media. Using the site map and search facility you can explore its various campaigns, publications, information services, conferences and research and development.

National Literacy Trust (UK)
http://www.literacytrust.org.uk/
The National Literacy Trust's web site and online database is provided free to help everyone concerned with promoting literacy in the UK to work collaboratively. Its work is supported by the Basic Skills Unit (see above).

On Course (UK)
http://www.uk-courses.co.uk/
On Course is dedicated to courses in London. It is crammed with articles and thousands of course listings. You can also access Study Abroad, a comprehensive site for students wishing to study overseas. It includes courses, colleges and universities in Britain, France, Spain, Australia and the USA.

Open College of the Arts (UK)
http://www.oca uk.com
The OCA is an educational trust providing home-based arts education. Courses include photography, creative writing, interior and garden design, visual arts and music. Some courses have university accreditation and credit points.

Pre-Retirement Association (UK)
http://www.pra.uk.com/enter.html
The PRA helps people plan for retirement or redundancy. They train trai-

ners to work as advisers. You can use the site to explore their publications and training videos.

SCRE Publications Catalogue (UK)
http://www.scre.ac.uk/cat/0947833269.html
This page gives information on *Adult Participation in Education and Training*, a book by Pamela Munn and Carolyn MacDonald. It reports the findings from a survey of about 2,000 adults on their attitudes towards returning to education and training. It identifies differences between returners and non-returners, and highlights factors affecting participation.

Scottish Further Education Unit (UK)
http://www.sfeu.ac.uk/
The aim of the site is to provide up-to-the-minute news, analysis and information indispensable to everyone involved in the Scottish FE sector.

Signposts to Lifelong Learning (UK)
http://signposts.hants.gov.uk/signposts/
This site offers a comprehensive directory of adult and continuing education courses in Hampshire, with a search function and contact key.

Workers' Education Association (UK)
http://www.wea.org.uk/
The WEA is the largest voluntary provider of adult education in the UK. It aims to provide access to a wide range of educational opportunities for the general public and specific target groups of students. You can link into courses, news, districts, tutoring, publications, global development, links and volunteering.

Fig. 43. The Workers Educational Association. The web site includes a handy selection of UK, European and international educational links.

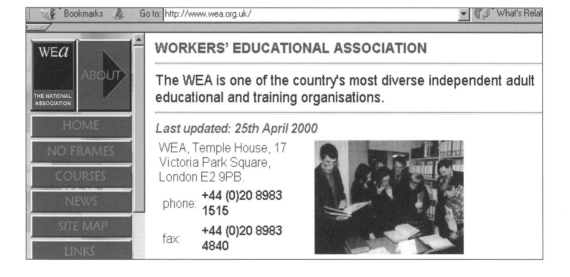

Online and distance adult learning providers

Amersham & Wycombe College (UK)
http://www.amersham.ac.uk/
The College offers online learning as well as traditional courses. Follow the link to online learning on its home page. The college is a partner in a project to address skills shortages in ICT in the Thames Valley region. Access to learning is through a virtual centre which uses ICT solutions to provide flexible and cost effective training. You can download learning modules to your home or work computer.

Australian Correspondence Schools (Australia)
http://www.qldnet.com.au/acs/
ACS says you can use the net to speed your studies in several ways. You can contact tutors who are on duty five days a week, to send in email assignments, to communicate with other students living locally or studying similar courses, to research for assignments via the net, and to download material from the school's database.

BBC Online (UK)
http://www.bbc.co.uk/home/today/
From the home page you can access Bitesize – homework help. You can also click onto Education and access schools, adult learning, education in the nations, resources and BBC knowledge.

Bell College of Technology (UK)
http://floti.bell.ac.uk/floti/default.htm
FLOTI stands for Flexible Learning on the Internet. FLOTI courses are awarded by the Scottish Qualifications Authority, the University of Strathclyde, the Open University, or the University of Hertfordshire. As a member of FLOTI you become a Bell College of Technology student which brings with it discounts from many suppliers.

Chemeketa Community College (USA)
http://bbs.chemek.cc.or.us/public/default.htm
This site has over eighty courses and four associate degrees online. The regular faculty teaches these courses and, on successful completion, credit courses can be used towards a certificate, degree or transfer.

College of Exploration (Bermuda)
http://www.coexploration.org/
The Bermuda-based College of Exploration creates and delivers distance learning and onsite courses, workshops and related resources, which offer opportunities for integrated learning about personal development, ecology, the environment, community, technology, and leadership. The components are administration, classrooms and seminar rooms, media centre and libraries, a personal reflection space, an assessment centre and a social centre. These integrated components use web-conferencing, chat, internet, email, OBDC databases, and assessment software in a seamless web-based interface.

Adult education sites ....

Continuing Education Network (USA)
http://www.tcen.com/learning
This site presents multimedia interactive audio-visual presentations that allow engaging and efficient learning. Its course catalogue covers a broad spectrum of subjects. There are over 200 tutorials to choose from with new course offerings and categories being added regularly. There are free 'try it before you buy it' demos for most of the courses.

Encarta Online (USA)
http://encarta.msn.com/find/Concise.asp?ti=0109B000
This Microsoft site focuses on adult education and provides links to articles, web sites, periodicals and news headlines. Further facilities include search, email and downloads.

Humber College Online (Canada)
http://hcol.humberc.on.ca/
This community college offers 135 full-time diploma and certificate programs at the post-secondary and post-diploma levels, as well as over 1,000 courses through continuing education. The online service provides a virtual environment for learning in any place at any time; select this link for information about interactive distance education courses.

Leicester Adult Education College (UK)
http://www.leicester-adult-ed.ac.uk/
You can access course information from the college in Leicester. There are more than 500 courses to choose from in their online prospectus.

Louisiana College Virtual Campus (USA)
http://lconline.lacollege.edu/
LC Online offers courses for college credit via the internet. Through a combination of taped lectures and online resources, it gives qualified non-traditional students a chance to obtain a college education while they pursue their normal work and family responsibilities.

Mercy College (USA)
http://MerLIN.Mercynet.edu/
This site provides online education with various undergraduate courses which can be taken without interfering with busy schedules. Using computers and modems, learners can access the MerLIN system when they have time to exchange electronic postings, files, email and internet-based information with instructors, classmates, and supporting staff.

North Seattle Community College (USA)
http://www.virtualcollege.org/
From the Virtual College page you can link into online courses (credited and non-accredited) and view course descriptions and schedules.

Online University Teaching Centers (USA)
http://eagle.cc.ukans.edu/~cte/OtherSites.html
Through this Kansas University site, you can access a very useful world-

wide listing of online resources in higher education. Most of the UK ones deal with academic staff development.

Plymouth College of Further Education Online (UK)
http://www.pcfe.ac.uk/learning/index.html
The College's Open Access Centre delivers the OCR Computer Literacy and Information Technology Certificate over the internet. Learners can experience interactive learning and at the same time learn how to use Microsoft's popular Office suite (Word, Access and Excel) without even leaving home. Its Faculty of Technology runs online courses in telecommunications including mobile phone and satellite communications. The material is presented using the latest Video Streaming techniques so you can view recorded lessons just as if you were in a classroom.

Sams Teach Yourself Online (USA)
http://www.styonline.com/
Sams is a leading US publisher of computer books and materials. Through this site you can link into an online classroom for computer technology. From the home page, you can access their catalogue, a free sample online course, and register as a student.

Sheffield College (UK)
http://www.sheffcol.ac.uk/
This is the web site of the UK's largest further education college. The site contains details of ten short accredited online training courses in four areas: introduction to learning on the internet, information retrieval on the world wide web, web page authoring, and online group working.

University of Oxford Department for Continuing Education (UK)
http://www.conted.ox.ac.uk/
OUDCE offers a wide range of educational and training programmes. 'You can study in Oxford, in the region, or online, for pleasure and an Oxford qualification.' The department currently runs the following distance learning courses using the internet as their main means of delivery: a Diploma in Local History, and a Certificate in Computing.

Virtual School of English (UK)
http://www.btinternet.com/~virtualschool/index.html
Published in Scotland, these pages offer courses in such topics as basic examination English, writers on the web, and creative writing.

Women's U (USA)
http://www.womensu.com
Based in New York State, Women's U claims to have been the first virtual educational community developed by, for, and about women. It offers a variety of teleclasses, taught by trained personal and business coaches, on topics such as financial prosperity, personal development, business building, spirituality, parenting, life transitions, and relationships.

Tour the Site

About Women's U.

About Our Classes

Meet the Faculty

Free Quote-Cards

Women's U.

Where Women Come Together for Information, Affirmation and Inspiration

● <u>Tour</u> the Site

● About <u>Women's U.</u>

● About Our <u>Classes</u>

Welcome to the First Virtual Learning Community for Women

We say "first" because there are sure to be others. Women have been gathering together to share wisdom and to gain insight from one another's experiences since the dawn of time. The idea of creating a sacred space where women can come together to guide, nourish and support one another through life challenges and transitions is nothing new--but the use of today's technology makes this possible in a way that our foremothers would never have anticipated.

Fig. 44. At Women's U, educational opportunities for women are but a mouse-click away.

Special interest courses

ESL Online (USA)
http://www.eslonline.com/
ESLonLine offers courses over the internet in English as a second language with emphasis on American usage and culture for the professional businessperson and others with an interest in learning and perfecting their skills in the English language. The courses are ideal for those who have completed a traditional English course and wish to maintain their English language skills through continued online practice.

Handwriting University (USA)
http://www.handwritingu.com
Visit the world's first and only virtual 'university' dedicated to the growth and understanding of handwriting analysis. Topics covered include handwriting analysis, self-improvement, and personal growth.

Language and Leisure (Ireland)
http://www.lingolex.com/iretran/index.html
You can access a language-training organisation operating language programmes in Ireland combined with leisure breaks through this site.

Learner Drivers (UK)
http://www.learners.co.uk/
Link to the UK directory of driving schools, residential driving schools and off-road training for under 17s. You can try the interactive theory test and visit the learners' shop.

Massachusetts Institute of Technology (USA)
http://web.mit.edu/course/21/21.japan/
You can link to online Japanese language courses for Japanese levels 1, 2, 3, 4 and 7 delivered via the web.

MiamiMOO (USA)
http://miamimoo.mcs.muohio.edu/
This site offers access to an educational 'MOO' (a virtual reality environment). Using computer-generated simulations, the students and instructors collaborate to reconstruct historical sites and re-enact the events that took place there.

Virtual Art School (UK)
http://dspace.dial.pipex.com/town/plaza/ad370/
The site offers a Core Graphics Course, exploring the purpose of graphic design and the means of creating effective design with the elements available to the graphic designer – space, shape, size, line, colour, texture. The course material is a blend of illustrations, animations, activities and case studies.

World Wide Language Institute
http://www.wwli.com/
This is a virtual language learning organisation which offers online courses in Mandarin Chinese, including a free sample lesson, translation centre and other resources.

Writers on the Net (USA)
http://www.writers.com/
This site offers classes, tutoring and mentoring, writers' groups. It is a group of published writers who are also experienced teachers. There are services here would be of value to poets, business writers, fiction writers, journalists, essayists, mystery writers, science fiction and fantasy writers, playwrights and screenwriters, horror writers, writers of historical fiction, and academic writers.

home
writing classes
tutoring
student quotes
subscribe
writers groups
faqs
newsletter
writing tips
bookstore
contests
contact us
register
writers forum

Writing School (Canada)
http://www.WritingSchool.com
Based in British Columbia, this is an online college-level school that teaches all aspects of writing: fiction, non-fiction, business writing, screenwriting, and academic writing.

Learning guidance providers

Learn Direct (UK)
http://www.learningdirect.org
This site gives access to free advice on learning and career matters. There is also a freephone helpline (0800 100 900).

Adult education sites ....

Fig. 45. Learn Direct. If you don't know where to look for a course, this site can help you; or telephone the free helpline.

Related chapters

Chapter 3 – University web sites
Chapter 4 – Vocational training web sites
Chapter 5 – Occupational training web sites
Chapter 7 – Distance and online learning web sites
Chapter 8 – Specialist web sites for particular groups

Related Internet Handbooks

Careers Guidance on the Internet, Laurel Alexander (Internet Handbooks).

7 Distance and online learning sites

In this chapter we will explore:

▶ *the practicalities of distance learning online*
▶ *distance and open learning organisations and links*
▶ *teaching and learning resources*
▶ *distance and online courses*

. . . .

The practicalities of distance learning online

Distance learning is where a course is facilitated normally by post and telephone, possibly with email and fax support. Material is usually delivered via text, video or tape. You, as the learner, are very much on your own with little or no interaction with other students and limited interaction with the tutor. Distance learning is a term used to define methods of learning that allows the learner to take charge of their programme of study. The student works at a time, place and pace suited to them. In order to do this, learners require a wide variety of material designed to take the tutor's place, providing specially prepared information and exercises. In order to support this learning, students should have access to a tutor (via post, phone or tutorial meetings) and to the choice of meeting with other students (e.g. summer schools, drop-in study centres).

Council for the Accreditation of Correspondence Colleges (UK)
CACC exists to develop a system of accreditation approved by the Department for Education and Employment. It is an independent body which inspects every aspect of a college and gives approval if the Council's criteria is met.

Fig. 46. The UK Open University. Students of Cognitive Psychology have been using internet video-conferencing to participate in tutorials and practical lab activities.

Distance and online learning sites ....

The Open University (UK)
This university requires no entry qualification (except for higher degrees).
You can fit in your studies around the rest of your life (75% of OU students
remain in full-time employment throughout their studies). Many students
are sponsored by their employers. On OU courses, students receive personal attention and support from their network of tutors and there are
opportunities to meet them and your fellow students in tutorials, self-help
groups and residential schools. The university actively encourages mature
students and has had more than 165,000 students of all ages and backgrounds obtain OU degrees. Further points of interest include:

1. the option of spreading your study over several years – with breaks
2. most students are part-time
3. degree courses contain a mixture of course units, notes, exercises,
   self-assessment tests, assignments, audio tapes, records, slides,
   videos, broadcasts, options to attend study centres and summer
   schools
4. non-degree courses are offered
5. the academic year runs from February to November
6. most learning is done through correspondence, radio, TV, audio-visual
   materials, workbooks and personal tutor contact
7. there is the option of self-standing materials.

Online learning
Online learning is computer-based. You receive assignments via email or
other internet facilities and you submit them the same way. You can
interact with student online, either in real-time or via newsgroups. You
can be part of online discussion groups. News can be posted to bulletin
boards. Tutor material can be downloaded from the internet. You can
access virtual libraries. You can access interactive computer applications
as part of your online learning. On top of your home computer, you could
have a video camera, as would other students on your course and all of
you would be linked to the tutor – this is called video-conferencing.
Conferences and seminars across the globe can be brought to your
virtual classroom by video.

▶ *Comment* – 'About 75 per cent of computer training takes place in
  classrooms, but within 3–5 years online and video-based training
  will account for 75 per cent.' (Microsoft).

Choosing a course
When choosing a course you need to ask yourself:

1. If I'm taking a qualification, is it widely recognised in the workplace?
2. What is the qualification offered and who is that accredited by?
3. What kind of facilities does the school have?
4. Will I be assessed by exam or by continuous assessment?
5. Are there any hidden financial extras in connection with the course?
6. Will I get to chat to fellow students?
7. What kind of tutorial support is there?

8. Is there a time limit for completion of the course?
9. Can they send me an example of specimen material?
10. When was the course material last revised?
11. Do they give refunds?
12. Are the tutors qualified?
13. Do I have the right hardware and software for online learning?

Studying at home
While studying at home has plenty of benefits, it also brings new challenges – and it requires you to have self-discipline!

(a) Finding a place to study
You will need to ensure you have a place to study. Ideally a specific room away from family bustle and people making requests would be good. But if that isn't possible, then try to make a special corner in the home for your study. If you are working online, where will your computer be? Don't forget you also need a space for books and paperwork. Will you need to battle for ownership of hands-on time with your children or partner?

(b) Working around the family
You will need to make boundaries when you want to study. Requests from family and friends will have to take second place. Getting into the habit of time management and timetabling should help. Explain to your family at the start what you are trying to do and why it is so important to you. Ask their co-operation so that they feel part of what is going on.

(c) Getting disciplined
There will be times when you will want to sit in the garden or go out for a drink. All study and no play makes Jack and Jill boring people – and prone to burnout. However, there will be times when you will have to be firm with yourself, ignore all temptations and get on with your study. When there are times like this, set yourself targets with a reward at the end.

(d) Keeping yourself motivated
Always keep in mind WHY you are studying. You're taking this course to get a better job, to improve your confidence, to make more money, to get promotion, to return to work – but most of all you are doing it because it is the right thing for you.

▶ *Comment* – 'Nine out of 10 large US companies have some on-line training in 1999. One day training for every job on earth will be available on the Net.' *The Financial Times*.

Distance and open learning organisations and links

American Center for the Study of Distance Education (USA)
http://www.cde.psu.edu/ACSDE/
ACSDE seeks to promote distance education research, study, scholarship, and teaching and to serve as a clearinghouse for the dissemination of knowledge about distance education.

Association of British Correspondence Colleges
http://www.west-midlands.com/abcc
The ABCC is a voluntary association of UK colleges which comply with a code of ethics guaranteeing standards of service and integrity in their dealings with students. The site includes a list of member colleges with hyperlinks and email addresses.

British Association for Open Learning (UK)
http://www.baol.co.uk/
This is an organisation for people involved in flexible training and development. From its home page, you can access membership details, BAOL conferences and events, learning centres, press releases and links.

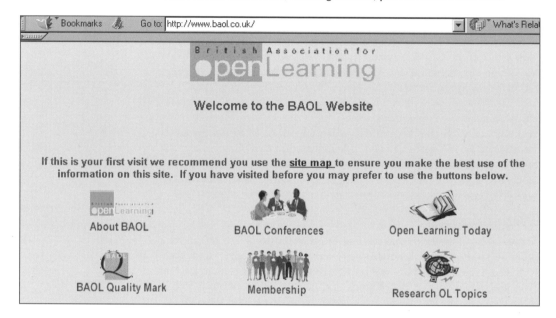

Fig. 47. The British Association for Open Learning (BAOL) exists to promote quality and best practice in open, flexible and distance forms of learning throughout the education and training sectors of the UK, Europe and internationally.

CommUnity (UK)
http://www.community.org.uk/
This site refers to the Computer Communicators Association that represents the interests of the UK online community. There is an ezine, press releases, details of meetings, documents and links.

Contact Consortium (USA)
http://www.ccon.org/
From this Californian site, you can access a broad range of information for contacts, culture and community in digital space, relating to the rise of new virtual worlds on the internet. The non-profit consortium supports special interest groups, holds conferences, sponsors research and papers, and serves as a catalyst for this new medium.

Continuing and Distance Education Links (USA)
http://www.cde.psu.edu/users/atb/main.htm
This site contains links to resources in the fields of continuing and dis-

tance education. From the home page you can link into computer support, distance education, instructional design resources, student resources and www information and much more.

Distance Education Online Symposium (USA)
http://www.cde.psu.edu/ACSDE/DEOS.html
DEOS was established by the American Centre for the Study of Distance Education at Penn State. The symposium comprises *DeosNews*, an electronic journal for distance educators, and DEOS-L, an electronic forum.

Distance Learning on the Net
http://www.hoyle.com/distance.htm
This is a useful page of links for online and distance learning – included are descriptions of distance education web sites, along with links to lead you to further distance learning and education resources on the net.

Fig. 48. Distance Learning on the Net.

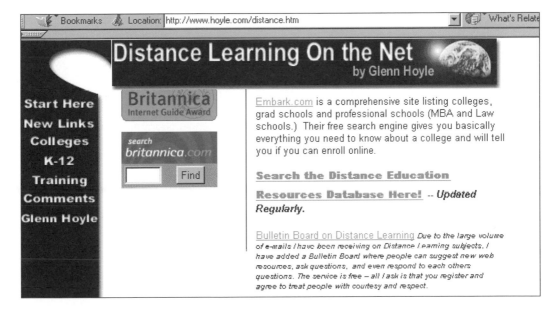

Electronic Emissary Project (USA)
http://www.tapr.org/emissary/
Based at the University of Texas at Austin, in the College of Education, the Electronic Emissary Project is an online matching service that helps teachers locate experts in different disciplines who use the internet and who are willing to engage in electronic exchanges with teachers and students.

Internet Relay Chat
news:alt.irc
If you are unfamiliar with IRC, check out this newsgroup for more information. IRC clients (software) are available for most personal computers and for Unix shell accounts. Just type this phrase into the location panel of your browser. This is one of several places to find out about internet relay chat (IRC). IRC channels allow internet users around the world to discuss

topics in real time. These users can be students, teachers, lecturers or tutors.

Knowledge Ability (UK)
http://www.knowab.co.uk/ka.html
This site provides access to consultancy in online communications, collaboration and learning. Its services include 'Working by Wire', an online course for building online virtual teams.

Learn Online
http://learnonline.micro.umn.edu/
This site reflects a project at the Digital Media Centre. It promotes the use of the internet and multimedia to enhance teaching and learning.

Learning over the Internet (USA)
http://www.unc.edu/cit/guides/irg-38.html
From the home page you can link to colleges, universities, and other educational institutions teaching classes or delivering course materials over the internet. Also included are consortia and other organisations devoted to delivering distance education with networked technologies.

Open and Distance Learning Quality Council
http://www.odlqc.org.uk/odlqc/
CACC was set up in 1968 as an independent body with the co-operation of the Secretary of State for Education and Science. It is the only organisation in the UK recognised as responsible for the award of accreditation to institutions offering distance education courses.

Open Forum (UK)
http://www.open-forum.co.uk/
This site provides explanations of distance learning issues, choosing courses plus a selection of UK institutions.

Open Learning Foundation (UK)
http://elgar.tvu.ac.uk/olf
The OLF is a membership organisation that collaborates with others to produce high quality learning materials, researches their best use, and provides a range of support to universities and colleges in the introduction of open learning. You can click on to a wide selection of options including information about OLF, publications, support, collaboration and news. When you have travelled to the options, there are links that take you to other related sites.

Consultancy

Training Place (USA)
http://www.trainingplace.com/source/thelist.html
This discussion list relates to the development of web-based training and online learning programs. There are links to registration, the daily digest, products, services and resources.

Teaching and learning resources

Blackboard Teachers Tool Box
http://company.blackboard.com/courseinfo/
This site powers the online teaching and learning environments at colleges, universities and K-12 school districts around the world. You can build and manage course web sites and online campus environments, without knowing of HTML or other programming languages. From the home page you can view product reviews, demos, technical specifications, contact points and buying. You can also find out about training, web hosting and support.

Convene (USA)
http://www.convene.com/
Convene designs and produces customised online programs for schools and colleges. Students can use virtually any computer with a modem to access their classes. Instructors interact with their students both individually and in groups, allowing them to give personal attention while maintaining important group dynamics. More than 50,000 students have completed some 250,000 courses using its software and services.

Distance Education and Technology (Canada)
http://demo.cstudies.ubc.ca/
Developed at the University of British Columbia, this page illustrates a number of software applications that can be used for delivering distance education courses over the internet. From the home page, you can click onto audio, conferencing, database, integrated, Java and testing.

eCollege (USA)
http://www.ecollege.com/
eCollege provides commercial technology and services enabling colleges and universities to offer an online environment for distance and on-

Fig. 49. eCollege. Its services include course development, instructional design, a student/faculty help desk, enrolment marketing, program consulting, and an in-house creative support group

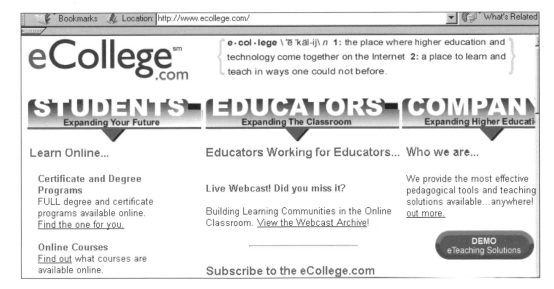

Distance and online learning sites ....

campus learning. It allows colleges and universities to outsource the creation, launch, management and support of an online education platform. It products include online campuses, courses, course supplements and support services, including design, development, management and hosting services, plus administration, faculty, and student support.

Eduprise (USA)
http://www.eduprise.com/
Eduprise provides a range of e-learning services to corporate training providers and higher education institutions.

EdSurf's Courses on the Net (USA)
http://www.edsurf.net/edshack/courses.htm
This is a useful online distance education learning resource for adult students. From the home page you can browse a selection of online courses or have a look at online computer training. There is a comprehensive search facility with links to virtual universities, virtual high schools, links and news. You can browse a selection of online courses dealing with the internet, computers, accounting, business, economics, education, English, languages, history, arts, science and social sciences.

EduTech (Switzerland)
http://tecfa.unige.ch/info-edu-comp.html
Edutech is a useful online resource for education and technologies. It offers a variety of options including sites of the month, an alphabetical search for themes, a query search, and an opportunity to submit a theme to Edutech's database.

Embanet (Canada)
http://www.embanet.com/
Embanet has developed a commercial virtual learning environment for MBA students, that they say combines affordability, high-value service and ease of use. It was developed, used and tested at the University of Toronto School of Management.

Get Educated (USA)
http://www.geteducated.com/
Get Educated publishes a free *Directory of Online Colleges, Internet Universities, & Training Institutes* so you can take a quick trip round the growing number of virtual campuses. If you can't find what you are looking for, check the free articles for distance learners' section of the resource centre. Get Educated publishes the *Virtual University Gazette* (VUG), a free email newsletter for distance learning professionals. If you are looking for a comprehensive guide to accredited virtual graduate schools, you can consult its *Best Distance Learning Graduate Schools: Earning Your Degree Without Leaving Home,*' published by the Princeton Review and Random House. This guide profiles around 200 graduate programs in the USA and abroad.

IntraLearn (USA)

http://www.intralearn.com/

The company produces and sells integrated online learning systems, enabling educators, trainers and individual corporate departments to rapidly create, deliver and manage secure, interactive and measurable learning over the Internet and corporate intranets.

Learning Sites (USA)

http://www.learningsites.com/

This site offers interactive online educational and research tools. It designs and develops interactive 3D models and virtual worlds for public school education, archaeological research, scholarly publication, and museum or archaeological site exhibition.

Lotus Learning Space (USA)

http://www.lotus.com/home.nsf/welcome/learnspace

Learning Space is a Lotus web-based product that integrates live, self-paced and collaborative learning into a single easy-to-use environment. By combining course content, technical, and educational services, organisations can gain the benefits of a complete distributed learning solution. The site includes a practical guide to developing performance-based, performance-assessed and collaborative online courses.

National Teaching and Learning Forum (USA)

http://www.ntlf.com/

The National Teaching and Learning Forum began publication in 1991 as a joint venture with the ERIC Clearinghouse on Higher Education. It is an online facility for colleagues to share new ways of helping students reach the highest levels of learning. There are icons leading to forums, the library, subscriptions, and a search facility.

| About NTLF |
| Subscribe/Renew |
| |
| Current Issue |
| Previous Issues |
| |
| Library |
| Special Features |
| Discussion Forum |

Open Learning Directory (UK)

http://www.bh.com/

This is a web site of Butterworth-Heinemann, international publisher of books, open learning materials and electronic products for students and professionals in technology, medicine and business. On the home page, you can link to the map or text links to enter the web site and find information specific to your continent.

Resources in Distance Education (USA)

http://ccism.pc.athabascau.ca/html/ccism/deresrce/de.htm

This is a web-based resource for the use of educational technology in distance education, initiated by Athabasca University. For the most part this database contains post-secondary resources on the web.

SERF (USA)

http://www.udel.edu/serf

Serf is a web-based distance education environment developed at the University of Delaware. Serf makes it possible to create and deliver courses in a self-paced multimedia learning environment that enables students to navigate a syllabus, access instructional resources, communicate, and submit assignments over the web. Serf uses relational databases which keep track of users, maintain states between interactions, deliver courses, and monitor student progress. There are databases for calendars, syllabuses, assignments, grades, rosters, and styles. When a user logs on, each database plays a part in creating the appropriate screen for the moment.

Symposium (USA)
http://www.centra.com/product/index.html
Centra 99 (incorporating Symposium) is an integrated system enabling live collaboration, covering ad hoc meetings, one-to-one meetings, marketing, product demonstrations and team collaboration, interactive seminars, large-scale presentations, and hands-on training sessions.

Tools for Developing Interactive Academic Web Courses (Canada)
http://www.umanitoba.ca/ip/tools/courseware/
This University of Manitoba site includes an excellent article that sets out a model for developing web-based teaching and learning in theory and practice, and very useful links to a comparison of online course software products.

Fig. 50. TopClass. Serving over 600 organisations, TopClass offers open authoring and content management, testing and certification, personalised courseware, and the use of discussion groups, mailing lists and video-conferencing.

TopClass (USA)
http://www.wbtsystems.com/
The TopClass system (version 4.0) is designed to support the management and delivery of courses over the web. It integrates threaded electronic mail and discussion groups, security, content assembly tools, testing and tracking features, customisation, and a host of other features to enable faculty members to create and manage courses easily and quickly. The company has offices in San Francisco, USA, and Dublin, Ireland.

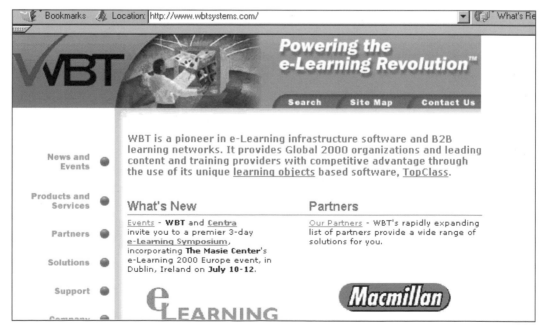

Tutor Pro (UK)
http://www.tutorpro.com
Based in Wellington, Somerset, Tutor Pro Ltd offers Tutornet, a delivery and tracking mechanism for training materials delivered over an intranet or the internet. You can edit, amend and add to its existing courseware, tailoring the courses to fit your own requirements. A sophisticated student management system lets you profile, manage and track training and support across your enterprise or user group.

UOL Publishing (USA)
http://www.uol.com/
UOL Publishing Inc. is a publisher of interactive, web-based courseware delivered through the internet or corporate intranets to the education and training market. It has a growing library of some 350 courses in management, computer applications, business, technical skills, and more; a VCampus including custom courseware development, web-based certification and testing, instructor training, and customisation of courses to meet clients' learning needs. It also offers courses on disk and CD-rom, classroom-based instruction, and custom print-based courseware development, publishing, and distribution.

Distance and online courses

Africa Growth Network
http://www.agn.co.za/
The Africa Growth Network is a distance learning organisation delivering training and education programmes via satellite. Its Global Access site has been designed for use with the Microsoft Internet Explorer 4.0 or above. It is an elaborately designed, graphically intensive and slow-loading site.

Bilston Campus (UK)
http://www.bilston.ac.uk/index.htm
This site is part of Wolverhampton College and offers distance and flexible learning courses in holistic therapy, learning and personal development, GCSE and A-levels, para-legal training and sports and leisure.

CAL Campus (USA)
http://www.calcampus.com/
The Computer Assisted Learning Centre (CALC) is a private, international education centre, which offers courses solely through the internet. Enrolment is open to all individual, mature learners. The complete CAL Campus catalogue is available to the public on the world wide web.

Clackamas (USA)
http://dl.clackamas.cc.or.us/
Distance learning courses offered here include internet classes, telecourses, and correspondence courses. You can access subjects such as IT, law enforcement, print reading, biology, and autocad. The site includes a workshop for anyone who has not taken an online course before.

Distance and online learning sites ....

Classroom Door (USA)

http://www.classroomdoor.com/

This site offers over 400 technical and 350 skills courses over the internet, relating to basic computing (Word, Excel, Quicken etc), professional and personal development, business applications, internet skills and technical skills.

Distance Education at a Glance (USA)

http://www.uidaho.edu/evo/distglan.html

This site from the University of Idaho guides educators through all phases of developing and delivering a course at a distance. The helpful guide of topics includes a useful overview, strategies for teaching at a distance, instructional development, evaluation, instructional television, instructional audio, computers, print, strategies for learning at a distance, research, interactive videoconferencing, the web copyright, and a glossary.

Distance Learning Environment (USA)

http://www.pathlore.com

Pathlore is a provider of computer-based enterprise training solutions worldwide. It delivers cross-platform computer-based training (CBT) and 'virtual classroom' solutions across corporate networks, intranets, and the Internet for large organisations. It also offers instructional design, courseware development, project management, and IT integration.

Distance Learning (UK)

http://www.distance-learning.co.uk/

In Association with the Open University, this contains details of international distance and open education and training opportunities. It gives access to the largest global database of distance and open learning courses. You can choose details of courses on: course providers, accountancy, finance and economics, applied science, arts and humanities, building and planning, business and administration, communications, computer science and information technology, education and training, examinations, law, leisure, management, medicine, pure science and maths and social sciences.

Globewide Network Academy (USA)

http://www.gnacademy.org/

Formed in Texas in 1993, GNA is an educational non-profit organisation whose aim is to assist in all aspects of virtual and distance learning. It produces an online distance education catalogue of more than 17,000 courses and programs. It also consults on the development of virtual organisations and training materials. You can visit the student or teacher lounge, visit the bookstore, link to academic support or contact them.

GP Learning Technologies (Canada)

http://www.trainingnow.com/

Here, you can browse the online course catalogue for the courses and topics that interest you. The catalogue provides course descriptions together with place and times of offering. The online training concept is first, and foremost, a self-paced learning experience. This means a student can proceed through the course at a pace appropriate to them. No longer does a slower student need to feel rushed, or an advanced student need to be held back by slower classmates.

Interactive Distance Learning Resource Site (USA)
http://idl.fsu.edu/
This is an internet-supported distance learning from Florida State University offering selected bachelor's degree programs. If you have an Associate of Arts degree or equivalent, you can earn an FSU bachelor's degree without moving to Tallahassee. There is a link for prospective students offering degree programs in computer science, information studies and software engineering. There are links to specific departments, to admissions and registrations and current course offerings. You can contact named individuals and have more information sent to you. Another link is for prospective mentors with further links into orientation and training, qualifications required and how to apply.

International Centre for Distance Learning (UK)
http://www-icdl.open.ac.uk/
This is a site of the Open University and the ICDL, concerned with research, teaching, consultancy, information and publishing. Its databases contain information on over 31,000 distance learning courses, mostly in the Commonwealth countries. You can find out about 1,000 institutions teaching at a distance worldwide, and some 11,000 abstracts of books, journal articles, research reports, conference papers, dissertations and other types of literature relating to all aspects of the theory and practice of distance education. From the home page you can access databases on literature, institutions and courses.

Fig. 51. The International Centre for Distance Learning, a project of the UK Open University.

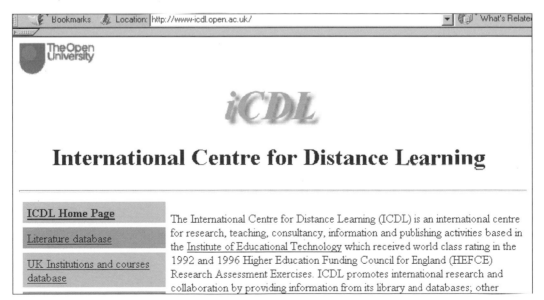

Distance and online learning sites ....

International Correspondence Schools (UK)
http://www.icslearn.com/
ICS is the largest distance learning training organisation in the world. During the last few years it has expanded its services to include home, business, and industry, but the service continues to be postal-based at the time of writing.

International School of Information Management (UK & USA)
http://www.isimu.edu/
ISIM is an accredited provider of distance education and training. It offers graduate degrees in business administration and information manage-ment. In addition to graduate degree programs, it offers corporate training programs, and classes for continuing education in various career-enhancing courses for the professional adult. You can use this site to learn more about ISIM and apply for admission online.

LearnLinc (USA)
http://www.ilinc.com
Developed in New York State, LearnLinc software is designed to facilitate live internet (online) learning. It involves an interactive, virtual classroom carried over the internet, corporate or university intranets, or wide area network environments. It says that more companies, governments, and universities use LearnLinc to deliver online training than any other live internet learning software in the world.

LifeLongLearning.com (USA)
http://www.lifelonglearning.com/
This site offers a database of distance learning courses, scholarships for online degrees, information on financing your lifelong learning and a specific section for adult learning resources.

McGraw-Hill Lifetime Learning (USA)
http://www.mhlifetimelearning.com/
This site offers internet courses, offline correspondence courses, print-based materials, computer-based training and multimedia, as well as courses for individuals and organisations.

National Extension College (UK)
http://www.nec.ac.uk
The NEC specialises in supported home study courses and learning re-sources for professionals. The home page has a multitude of buttons. The bright green section is split into three sections. One has several icons related to NEC (e.g. contacts and equal opportunities). The second column has icons related to their learning programme divisions (e.g. courses and student information, and the third links you into the learning resources division (e.g. tutor/training resources). The sky blue icons down the left side take you into NEC press releases, partnerships and recruitment. Yet another icon links you to NEC News.

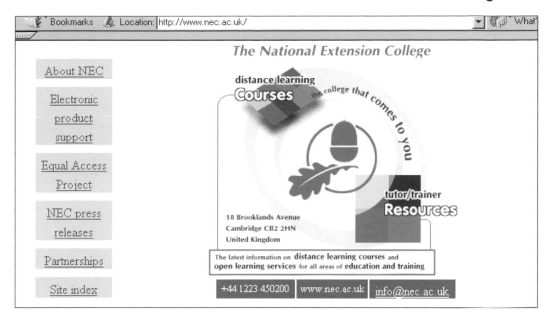

Fig. 52. The UK National Extension College. Its web site includes details of its project Equal Access to Open Learning (EATOL), and various forms of electronic support for students.

OnLine Training (USA)
http://www.oltraining.com/
Online Training Inc. offers free consultation over the phone to help you develop ways to use the internet for distributing training and information. From the home page you can access online courses, student services, income and career opportunities and contact points.

Open Learning Australia (Australia)
http://www.ola.edu.au/
OLA offers all Australians, regardless of age, location or educational qualifications, the opportunity to study university and TAFE (Tertiary & Further Education) units leading to diplomas, degrees and other qualifications.

Open Learning Agency of British Columbia (Canada)
http://www.ola.bc.ca/
OLA is a fully accredited publicly funded educational organisation and provides a wide range of formal and informal educational and training opportunities for learners around the world. Through its Open University, it has established collaborative bachelor programs in British Columbia.

PBS Adult Learning Service Online
http://www.pbs.org/als/college/
Here you can enrol in a telecourse and take college-credit courses, offered by colleges, universities, and public TV stations nationwide.

Peterson's (USA)
http://www.petersons.com/
This site is a leading US educational information provider connecting individuals, institutions, and corporations through books, software, net-

working services, online activities, and admissions services. From the home page you can link to college search, financial aid, online applications, more than 35,000 graduate study programs, distance learning courses, summer camps, student resources, press releases, contacts and downloadable data.

Rapid Learning (USA)
http://www.jobsecurity.com/courses.htm
These free, online courses help speed the learning process by defining the terminology necessary to the technology.

Student Awarded Scholarships International (USA)
http://www.sascholarships.com
This is a site for students who would like to further their education in law or business administration by means of distance learning. External joint degree programmes are provided by the National Association of Paralegals of England and the Southern Eastern University of America and any other universities included in the programme. You will find this a clear site offering information about scholarships, participating institutes, Q&As, plus contacts.

Trdv-Aus (Australia)
http://cleo.murdoch.edu.au/gen/trdev-aus/trdev_courses.html
This is a vocational education and training site with hyperlinks to a large number of online courses and related resources in Australia and New Zealand and many other countries. There is also a publications link.

University of Hull: Merlin (UK)
http://www.hull.ac.uk/merlin/
Merlin is a web-based learning environment that combines many of the advantages of face-to-face learning with the best of open and distance learning. It provides a tailorable, user-friendly environment for online course delivery, teaching and learning support, resource development and collaborative working. It welcomes approaches from HE and FE institutions, training providers, schools and colleges interested in consultancy, development and course hosting on Merlin.

Related chapters

Chapter 3 – Higher education online
Chapter 4 – Vocational training web sites
Chapter 5 – Occupational training web sites
Chapter 10 – Your own education and training web site

Related Internet Handbooks

The Internet for Students, David Holland (Internet Handbooks).

Fig. 53. Merlin's web-based learning environment is exclusively based on servers at the University of Hull. It welcomes approaches from HE and FE institutions, training providers, schools and colleges interested in consultancy, development and course-hosting.

8 Specialist sites for particular groups

In this chapter we will explore:

▶ *unemployed people*

▶ *young people*

▶ *disabilities*

▶ *special needs*

▶ *rehabilitation*

. . . .

Unemployed people

Education and Training (UK)
http://www.lifelonglearning.co.uk/etda/p2302.htm
This is a DfEE site giving access to education and training opportunities for New Deal at age 25 plus (those who have been unemployed for two years or more).

Fig. 54. Scottish Enterprise is broadly concerned with economic development in Scotland. It seeks to create innovative organisations, encourage learning and enterprise within an inclusive society, and the development of Scotland as a competitive location.

New Deal (UK)
http://www.newdeal.gov.uk/
New Deal is a key part of the UK government's 'welfare to work' strategy and this site offers information on training opportunities for New Deal jobseekers and employers.

Scottish Enterprise (UK)
http://www.scottish-enterprise.com/
Training for Work is an adult training programme available to people aged

18 or over who have been registered unemployed for six months or more. For some people, such as former offenders and those with special needs, this rule is waived.

Spark of Genius Training (UK)
http://www.sparkofgenius.co.uk/
This site provides links to help unemployed people who are involved in New Deal back to work using training, the internet and stand-alone software.

Training for Work (UK)
http://www.bstec.broadnet.co.uk/adults.htm
Birmingham & Solihull TEC's customised Training for Work programme offers the chance of specialised training for real jobs. The programme is open to anyone aged 25 or more who has been unemployed for at least six months. Customised training is available across a wide range of occupational sectors.

TUC (UK)
http://www.merseyworld.com/bfs/ie/tucb.ndeal.html
You can find a briefing on this site about what the New Deal means for older unemployed people.

Young people

Brathay (UK)
http://www.brathay.org.uk/
Brathay is an educational charity that provides residential outdoor training for young people (and industry). The site gives details of access courses, initiatives, trainer training, research, conferences, newsletter and links.

European Commission: Education, Training and Youth
http://europa.eu.int/comm/education/info.html
This site links into initiatives, strategic reflections, projects, press releases, information, search and feedback.

Sail Training Association (UK)
http://www.sta.org.uk/sta/
The STA is a youth charity which organises the annual *Cutty Sark* tall ships races and provides adventure sail training on the high seas for young people aged 16 to 24 aboard the famous tall ships the *Malcolm Miller* and the *Sir Winston Churchill*.

YMCA Training (UK)
http://www.ymca.org.uk/guides/ymca-2000/training.html
YMCA Training is one of the UK's largest national training organisations. It has been providing training in a caring environment for more than 35 years. It works with individuals, organisations and the community at more than 100 locations. It supplies NVQ training for young people along some 20 different vocational routes, and training for 21,000 un-

employed adults each year in job-seeking skills. It also offers training for organisations, especially in the voluntary sector. It offers vocational qualifications, short certificated courses such as basic health and safety and emergency first aid, and personal development training.

Disabilities

BBC Education Betsie Home Page (UK)
http://www.bbc.co.uk/education/betsie/
Betsie stands for the BBC Education Text to Speech Internet Enhancer. This is a system that allows blind and visually impaired people to listen to BBC web sites by using a screen reader that converts online text into speech. This site explains how it all works, with links to Betsie-enhanced pages.

Fig. 55. Disability and Information Systems in Higher Education deals with web development, distance learning, legal issues, computer-based courseware development, C&IT policy, and the support of disabled staff and students with technology.

Disability Net (UK)
http://www.disabilitynet.co.uk/info/education/index.html
From the home page, you can access some useful national and international links to education and training and archive material.

DISinHE (UK)
http://www.disinhe.ac.uk/
DISinHE stands for Disability Information Systems in Higher Education. It is a directory of organisations and companies which supply services and products for disabled students throughout the UK.

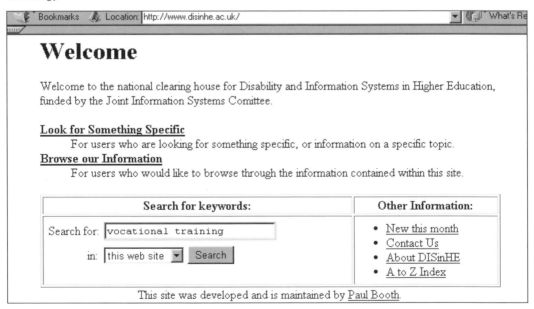

Dorton Training Services (UK)
http://www.rlsb.or.uk/reader/dts.html
This is a web site of the Royal London Society for the Blind. There are 10 links on this simple page: training opportunities, employment skills, tech-

nology centre, partnerships, enrolment, testimonials and contacts. It offers RSA NVQs, City & Guilds, ESOL, communication skills, Braille reading and writing skills, IT, and mobility and orientation skills.

Down's Syndrome Educational Trust (UK)

http://www.downsnet.org/downsed/

The Down's Syndrome Educational Trust is a charitable company whose main areas of activity include research, advice and consultancy to parents and others involved in the care and education of children with Down's syndrome. Its services include publishing and training (including correspondence courses).

Hereward College (UK)

http://www.hereward.demon.co.uk/

This college provides a friendly and informal environment for learning. If you have a disability and find that your local college cannot give you access to the course of your choice, Hereward can provide residential accommodation, and help in developing independent living skills. It provides access courses in television production, environmental science and media studies and is particularly geared to supporting adult returners.

Karten CTEC Centre (UK)

http://www.ctec.org.uk/index.html

The Karten CTEC Centre, a registered charity, is one of the UK's leading suppliers of computer-aided training and education to disabled people, to people with special needs, and to people with learning disabilities. It trains people in the use of computers and associated specialist hardware and software. It supports teachers working with disabled people, carers of the disabled, advocates of disabled people and relatives of the disabled.

Special needs

Adults with Learning Difficulties

http://www.niace.org.uk/publications/

NIACE publishes a book entitled *Adults With Learning Difficulties: Education for Choice and Empowerment: A Handbook of Good Practice.* It covers self advocacy and citizen advocacy, learning choices, ways and means of learning, learning for a purpose, integration, students with learning difficulties and additional complications, transition to community living, education of the wider community and issues for managers and planners.

After School Tuition (UK)

http://www.after-school-tuition.co.uk/

Through this site, you can access private tutoring services for children, adults, groups, business people and people with special learning needs. The company also offers various support services to schools, including multimedia publications and teaching aids.

Specialist sites for particular groups.....................................

Baskerville Online (UK)
http://www.baskervillenet.freeserve.co.uk/
This is the site of a school in Birmingham for children with special educational needs, mainly autism, but who are also experiencing other learning difficulties and challenging behaviour. It accepts pupils between the ages of 11 and 19.

Better Books (UK)
http://www.betterbooks.co.uk/
This is a useful online catalogue featuring more than 700 books dealing with special educational needs and learning disorders. Among the topics covered are dyspraxia, autism and dyslexia.

Britesparks (USA)
http://www.britesparks.com/
This web site has been developed for families and teachers of gifted children with special needs. It aims to provide a community atmosphere with handy resources, documents, a children's area, educational resources, a large number of clearly presented links to international organisations, and message boards for children and parents.

British Dyslexics (UK)
http://www.dyslexia.uk.com/
This site will give you access to experts who are interested in helping children and teenagers to succeed in compulsory further and higher education, and who also believe that getting extra help should not depend on a parent's ability to pay for extra tuition.

Class Consultants – Chartered Psychologists (UK)
http://www.class-consultants.co.uk/
You can access a group of psychologists, specialist teachers and education law advisors who specialise in special educational needs through this site. They advise parents, schools and other professionals with children who suffer from autism, Aspergers syndrome, attention deficit disorder, dyslexia and dyspraxia.

Conductive Educational Support Services (UK)
http://homepages.tesco.net/ ~ derek3/
This site offers courses for children and adults who suffer from cerebral palsy. The courses are held at Brockenhurst, Hampshire.

Educational Assessment of Able Children (UK)
http://www.btinternet.com/ ~ leecorbin/
This is an assessment and counselling service for able or gifted children and their parents. Local education authority INSET courses are also available.

Jenefer Roberts (UK)
http://www.jenefer.madhousenet.co.uk/
This site offers information about a range of activity and educational

products developed for babies and young children with little or no vision or profound learning disabilities by Jenefer Roberts, a teacher of visually impaired youngsters in Suffolk. These products have been recognised by the Royal National Institute for the Blind and added to their schools catalogue.

LD Pride Online (USA)
http://www.ldpride.net/
LD Pride is an interactive community for youth and adults with learning disabilities and attention deficit disorder. It enables them to interact with other learning disabled or ADD people. There is a chat room, bulletin board, useful links and an interactive 'learning style' section.

LD Online (USA)
http://www.ldonline.org/index.html
From the home page, you can access information about learning disabilities and disorders, attention deficit disorder, dyslexia, speech disorder, reading difficulties and special education. The information is aimed at parents, teachers, psychologists and paediatricians. There are hyperlinks to finding help, events, KidZone, an online newsletter, videotapes, an 'ask the expert' bulletin board, audio clips, and search facility.

Learning Disabilities Chat
http://chat.lycos.com/go.html?area=Life&room=Learning%20Disabilities
This is a chat room, hosted at Lycos, where you can make new friends online. You can chat here about learning disabilities, using either your true name or anonymously. Free registration is required.

National Association for Special Educational Needs (UK)
http://www.nasen.org.uk/mainpg.htm
NASEN is the leading organisation in the UK that aims to promote the education, training, advancement and development of all those with special educational needs. It has some 10,000 members and reaches a huge readership through its two journals: *British Journal of Special Education* and *Support for Learning*, and its magazine *Special!* There are links to research, press releases, consultation papers, events, books, contact details and membership.

News On Leisure (UK)
http://www.netcomuk.co.uk/~dobo/newson.htm
This site provides leisure information for children and adults with learning difficulties. This includes a diary of daily and weekly events such as drama, dance and gymnastics. There is also a links page and contact points.

NISS (UK)
http://www.niss.ac.uk/admin/sp-needs.html
National Information Services and Systems is a well-known and substantial portal site for UK higher education. It is a division of EduServ and receives funding with additional support from Sun Microsystems and Sybase. This page is specifically intended for those with, or working in

the area of, special needs or disabilities, particularly in higher education. It features a large number of useful links.

Otterhayes Trust (UK)
http://www.users.globalnet.co.uk/ ~ jcall/
Through this site you can find out about residential accommodation for 15 people with learning disabilities. The charity also provides educational and vocational training for residents at a centre in east Devon.

Pennine Camphill Community (UK)
http://www.penninecom.freeserve.co.uk/
Here you can access information about the 'therapeutic community' in Wakefield, West Yorkshire. It offers day and residential courses, and work for adults and young people with learning difficulties and special needs. Pennine's main work supports a therapeutic community that supports a College of Further Education and training for young people with special needs. There are about 45 students, both day and residential, alongside 28 co-workers and their families.

Special Education Resources on the Internet (USA)
http://www.hood.edu/seri/serihome.htm

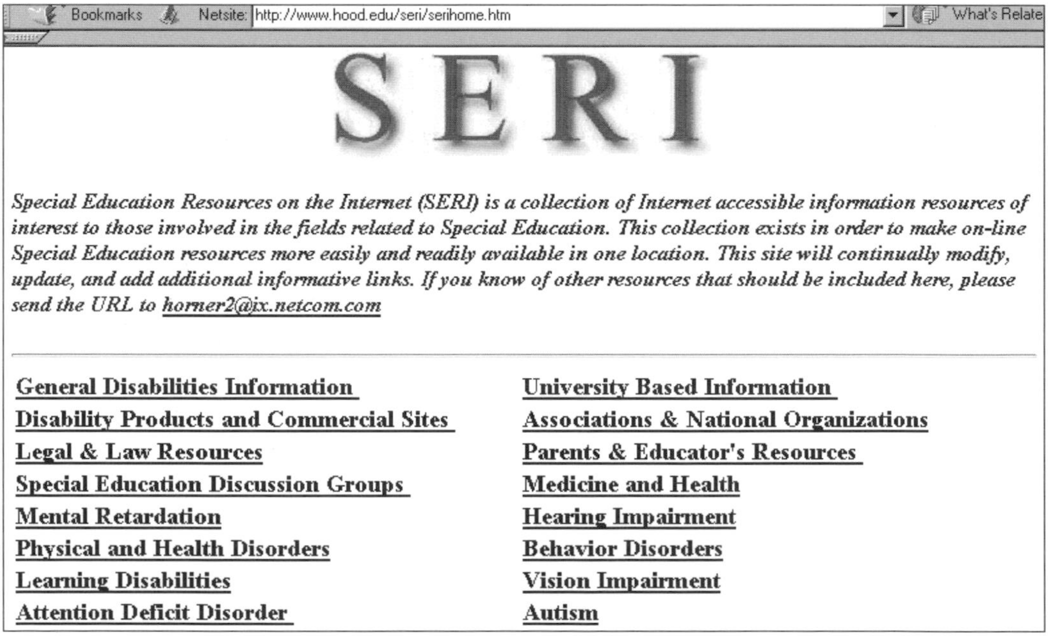

Fig. 56. Special Education Resources on the Internet (SERI). The site is hosted at Hood College in the USA.

SERI is a collection of net-based information resources for people involved with special education. There are links to special needs and technology, mental retardation, hearing impairment, behaviour disorders, learning disabilities, vision impairment, ADD, autism, speech impairment, and gifted children.

Netsite: http://www.hood.edu/seri/serihome.htm

SERI

Special Education Resources on the Internet (SERI) is a collection of Internet accessible information resources of interest to those involved in the fields related to Special Education. This collection exists in order to make on-line Special Education resources more easily and readily available in one location. This site will continually modify, update, and add additional informative links. If you know of other resources that should be included here, please send the URL to horner2@ix.netcom.com

General Disabilities Information	**University Based Information**
Disability Products and Commercial Sites	**Associations & National Organizations**
Legal & Law Resources	**Parents & Educator's Resources**
Special Education Discussion Groups	**Medicine and Health**
Mental Retardation	**Hearing Impairment**
Physical and Health Disorders	**Behavior Disorders**
Learning Disabilities	**Vision Impairment**
Attention Deficit Disorder	**Autism**

Special Educational Needs (UK)
http://www.dfee.gov.uk/sen/senhome.htm
This official site of the Department for Education & Employment aims to provide advice and materials for teachers, parents and others interested in or working with children with special educational needs. You can also search other sections of the National Grid for Learning (NGFL).

Special Needs and ICT (UK)
http://www.chilternweb.co.uk/senit/
From the home page, you can link into guidance for teachers about software or devices that will help their work with 'special needs' pupils.

Spellwell Software (UK)
http://wkweb4.cableinet.co.uk/spellwell/
From this page you can access software designed to help people suffering from dyslexia or other spelling and numeracy difficulties. There is an introduction to what's available, and a trial version you can download.

Underachievement Report (USA)
http://www.ascd.org/pubs/el/rimm.html
This is a report by a psychologist which offers help for teachers and parents in their efforts to ensure the success of their children.

Rehabilitation

DIMITRA (Greece)
http://www.dimitra.gr/aboutuk.htm
DIMITRA's vocational training programmes are aimed at long-term Greek unemployed youth of an average or higher educational level, people threatened by unemployment, business employees, people with physical or sensory disabilities, long-term unemployed women and people threatened by social exclusion. It develops multimedia technology and telematic networks for the support of training by distance and teleworking.

National Clearinghouse of Rehabilitation Training Materials (USA)
http://www.nchrtm.okstate.edu/
This site offers training resources and links to disability resources, health issues, mental health resources, special education, international disability links, disability research, 'reading room' and rehab links.

Paula's Special Education Resource Directory (USA)
http://www.conknet.com/~p_bliss/tbivocational.htm
This site is aimed at vocational preparation for students with traumatic brain injury and offers useful links for special education. From the home page you can explore various links to curriculum activities, teaching tools, and a contact.

PEARLS (UK)
http://www.brecon.co.uk/local/pearls/
PEARLS stands for Providing Education, Accommodation and Real Life

Specialist sites for particular groups.....................................

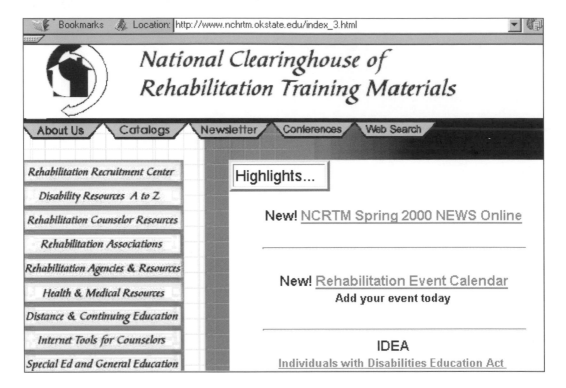

Fig. 57. The National
Clearing House of
Rehabilitation Training
Materials.

Skills. The charity – based in Swansea, south Wales – outlines its work with the homeless and with mentally and emotionally disturbed young people.

Speedwell Project (UK)
http://ourworld.compuserve.com/homepages/NOTE/
The Speedwell Project is a London-based work rehabilitation project. It provides vocational training, support and advice for unemployed people with a history of mental health problems. Its primary aim is to facilitate the reintegration of its students into mainstream education, training and employment. From the home page you can visit NetWork News, a feature which has been put together by students.

Related chapters

9 The best of the rest

In this chapter we will explore:

▶ *educational exchanges*
▶ *educational technology*
▶ *finance*
▶ *general*
▶ *information and links*
▶ *learning*
▶ *media and broadcasting*
▶ *professional development*
▶ *young people and students*

Introduction

This section is a bit of a lucky dip. Most of the sites don't fit into previous categories, either because of the subject nature or because they cross several boundaries. There is a selection from across the board, which have been chosen because of their interest value to educators.

Educational exchanges

The Central Bureau for Education Visits and Exchange (UK)
http://www.britcoun.org/cbeve/
A division of the British Council, the Central Bureau administers the UK side of a huge range of international education and training exchange

Fig. 58. The Central Bureau for Educational Visits & Exchanges is a division of British Council. It offers opportunities for pupils, students, teachers, trainers, lecturers and administrators in the UK education and training sectors.

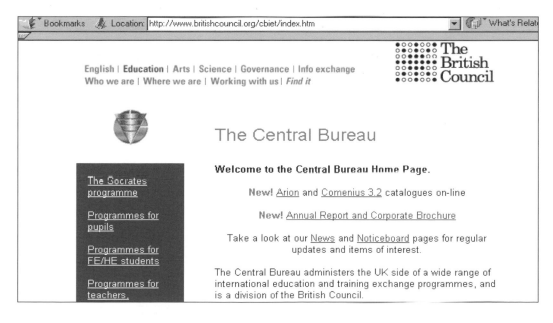

programmes. It offers opportunities for pupils, students, teachers, trainers, lecturers and administrators in the UK education and training sectors.

Educational technology

Association for the Advancement of Computing in Education (USA)
http://www.aace.org/
AACE is an international, educational, and professional organisation dedicated to the advancement of the knowledge, theory, and quality of learning and teaching at all levels with information technology. From its home page you can hyperlink to conferences, publications, membership, projects, grants, IT jobs, corporate participation, forums and contacts. The site is aimed at researchers, developers, and practitioners in schools, colleges, and universities, trainers, adult educators, and other specialists in education, industry and the government.

Association for Educational Communications and Technology (USA)
http://www.aect.org/
AECT's aim is to provide leadership in educational communications and technology by linking together professionals with a common interest in using educational technology and applying it to the learning process. The home page leads to publications, chapters, awards, employment opportunities and professional development.

Asynchronous Learning Networks (USA)
http://www.aln.org
In the Product Web area, you will find an online discussion of products used in the practice of ALN. It has created product-grouping forums that are the same as the groups shown in the product listing area of this web. Its product listings cover conferencing systems, graphics, multimedia (audio and video), web editing, question making, authoring, information management system evaluation, hardware, and miscellaneous tools for web-based teaching.

BBC Education: Webwise (UK)
http://www.bbc.co.uk/education/webwise/
Here you will find more than 1,000 pages of help, advice, and plain-speaking news on what you need to get the best out of the net, whatever your level of experience.

British Educational Communications and Technology Agency (UK)
http://www.becta.org.uk/
BECTA's remit is to ensure that technology supports the DfEE's drive to raise educational standards, and in particular that professional expertise is used to support the National Grid for Learning. From the home page you can go to magazine, projects, resources, support providers, archives, an online bookshop and press information. You can also access a site map and carry out a search from the home page.

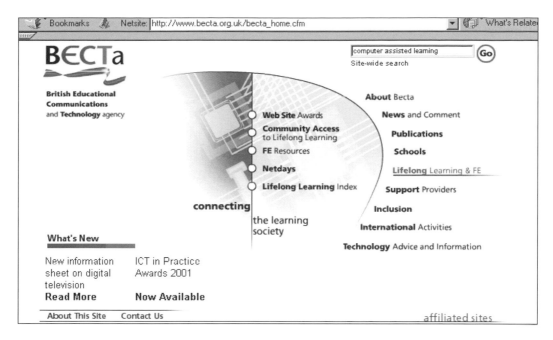

Fig. 59. The British Educational Communications and Technology Agency (BECTA).

BVG Software Training (UK)
http://www.careertrack.com/
This is site is aimed at corporate IT departments, professional and end user individuals. Its courses are deliverable by video, CD-rom, LAN (local area networks) and intranet.

Educational Technology
http://www.h-net.msu.edu/ ~ edweb/
EdTech paves the way for discussing the future directions of technology in education for many universities and school districts. This page shows how to subscribe to the EdTech list so that you receive messages in your email. The discussions on EdTech are archived by month, and organised by author, date, subject and thread.

SmartForce (USA)
http://www.smartforce.com/
Here you will find some pre-packaged tutorial software. A plug-in is required to view courses with a web browser. They only make Windows 95 and Windows NT versions of this plug-in. They have announced no plans to create a Mac version but plan to release a UNIX solution; 'CBT Campus' administration software/interface also available to co-ordinate delivery to students. This Californian company also has offices in England (West Drayton).

Columbia University Institute for Learning Technologies (USA)
http://www.ilt.columbia.edu/
The Institute aims to advance the role of computers and other information technologies in education and society. With school-based projects it

develops real-world projects using multimedia and network technologies to build sophisticated learning environments. In addition, it offers consulting and development services to educational and cultural institutions, government entities, and business and corporate bodies.

Electronic Publishing Association (USA)
http://www.epaonline.com/
The EPA is an international association of independent companies dealing with electronic publishing on CD-rom, DVD-rom and internet (plus localisation, marketing, production, sales and distribution). From its home page you can find out about its international membership. Its courses are related to learning languages. There is a demo icon on the home page to give a taster, as well as Q&As and contacts.

Integrated Management Resources (USA)
http://www.imr.on.ca/
IMR develops customised internet training programs to help people become better users of their computers and the internet. It teaches skills in library research, technology, teaching and communications. There are links to courses, a newsletter, feedback, links and trainer freebies.

Individual Software (USA)
http://www.individualsoftware.com/corporate/cbtproducts.htm
Individual Software's computer-based software tutorials are interactive, self-paced training programs designed to help the novice, intermediate, and experienced user to get the most out of their PC and PC applications. The courses on offer cover Windows, DOS and Macintosh.

Fig. 60. The Institute for Computer Based Learning, part of the Learning Technology Centre at Heriot-Watt University in Scotland.

Institute for Computer Based Learning (UK)
http://www.icbl.hw.ac.uk/
ICBL uses learning technology to provide solutions for higher education and industry. You can link to flexible learning, disseminations and simula-

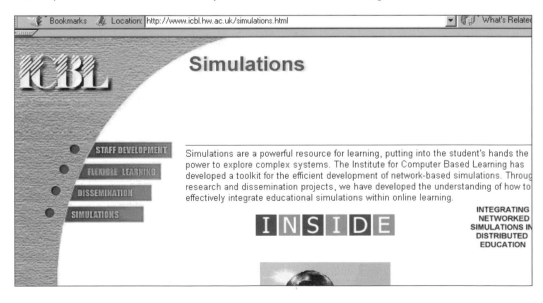

tions. ICBL is part of the Learning Technology Centre at Heriot-Watt University.

Knowledge Navigators (Canada)
http://www.knav.com/
Knowledge Navigators is an internet education infrastructure company. It supplies 'bolt-on' learning services to portals, online communities and organisations to enable online learning. Its core technology, Learning Engine, enables training departments, schools, and professional associations to create and deliver training and education to their employees and students. There are links to a resource library, events and contacts.

Microsoft Training & Certifications (USA)
http://microsoft.com/train_cert/
On this official MicroSoft site you can find out about training and certification courses, and link into MicroSoft courses, exams and training providers. Additional icons lead you to what's new, books, a newsletter, curriculum, and various international sites.

National Computing Centre (UK)
http://www.ncceducation.co.uk/
The NCC was formed by the UK government in 1966 to stimulate the use of computers through information, guidance and training. Today, NCC Education Services is one of the world's biggest independent IT training organisations. It supports some 400 training organisations in 30 different countries, with 25,000 students receiving its qualifications each year.

Oracle Learning Architecture (USA)
http://www.oracle.com
Oracle Corporation is one of the world's top software and database companies, and a provider of state-of-the-art global ebusiness solutions. There are loads of options from the home page: products, services, partners, employment, hot topics, internet seminars, webcasts, announcements and press releases. There is a search facility, contact details, and a free download area.

SCOLA (USA)
http://aaswebsv.aas.duke.edu/languages/langlab/scola.html
SCOLA is a non-profit educational consortium that receives and re-transmits television programmes from 50 different countries in their original languages. These programmes are transmitted via satellite to schools, colleges, universities, government and military installations, cableTV systems, independent TV stations, businesses and private individuals throughout north America and much of the northern and western hemisphere.

Trace Research and Development Center (USA)
http://www.tracecenter.org
Trace is a research centre at the University of Wisconsin. It focuses on making off-the-shelf technologies and systems involving computers, the

internet, and information kiosks. From its home page you can access an electronic library, industry support, education and user information.

University for Industry (UK)
http://www.ufiltd.co.uk/front.htm
UFI is a public-private partnership designed to boost the competitiveness of business and the employability of individuals. Working with businesses and education and training providers, it promotes modern technologies to make learning available at home, in the workplace and through a national network of learning centres. It hopes to provide information and advice to 2.5 million people a year by 2002, and create demand for up to one million courses and learning packages a year by 2004 – to be met by the UFI network and existing learning providers. The site contains numerous links to centres, news features, and resources.

University of Wales Learning Technology Development (UK)
http://toomol.bangor.ac.uk/
The UK IMS Centre, in partnership with the Open University, represents the UK on the international Instructional Management Systems Project, developing standards for learning technology systems.

Finance

Best Grants Database in Britain (UK)
http://www.enterprise.net/cds/grants/
This one-page site offers an 'enterprise in education' database of UK and European Union business grants, in use in over 200 colleges and universities in the UK. The database has details of over 300 grants from the EU plus over 1,000 other grants available from the UK government. There are also details of grants available from Training and Enterprise Councils, and local authorities. There is a separate grants database for Scotland.

Laura Ashley Foundation (UK)
http://www.users.dircon.co.uk/~laf/
Set up by the late Laura and Sir Bernard Ashley, the Foundation has helped hundreds of people to 'realise their potential and release talent'. Those helped include students of music, drama, ballet and conservation, and 'low achievers' needing a bit of a boost.

Scholarships & Financial Aid – Mach2 search (USA)
http://www.collegenet.com/mach25/
Mach25 claims to be the 'fastest scholarship search on the web, and it's free!' As you search, you can add and remove potential awards from your own customised list, and review or change your scholarship shortlist any time under password protection.

Student Loan Funding (USA)
http://www.studentloanfunding.com/
For parents and students, this site leads you to loan information, and for counsellors information about online loan counselling.

··· The best of the rest

General

Centre for Information and Language Teaching (UK)
http://www.cilt.org.uk/
CILT is an independent charitable trust, supported by central government grants, which aims to collect and disseminate information on all aspects of modern languages and their teaching. From the home page you can link into the UK network, projects, research, publications, resources, and various language conferences and courses.

Character Training International (USA)
http://www.character-ethics.org/
CTI provides workplace ethics training based on personal character, integrity, and the work ethic. You can link into information about its training courses, company overview, news and articles, and contact points.

Information and links

America's LearningeXchange (USA)
http://www.alx.org/
Here you can search for classroom courses, distance learning opportunities, web- and computer-based training, educational programs, conference workshops, and seminars. There are additional links to America's Job Bank and America's Career InfoNet.

Fig. 61. America's Learning eXchange (ALX) connects users to career development, training education and employment resources to remain competitive in today's workforce.

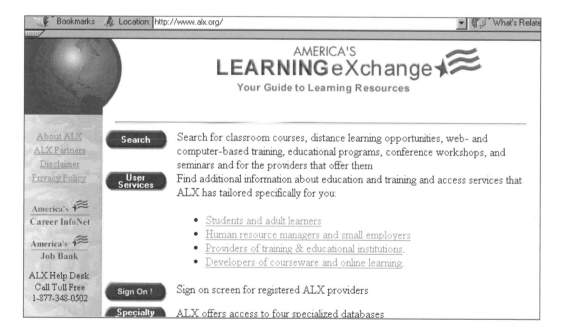

Asiaco (Singapore)
http://search.asiaco.com/
This site can provide information on almost anything to do with Asia, including education and vocational training schools.

British Accreditation Council (UK)
http://www.the-bac.org/
BAC was independently set up in 1984 'to improve and enhance the standards of independent further and higher educational institutions in the United Kingdom by the establishment of a system of accreditation'. It publishes a list of about 100 independent colleges which have been inspected and accredited, and which can be viewed on this site. It also has an online database where you can find information on all BAC accredited institutions by name, location, courses and special features, as well as links to their internet sites and email services.

Campaign for Learning (UK)
http://www.campaign-for-learning.org.uk/home.htm
The Campaign for Learning is a national charity, working to create an appetite for learning in individuals which will sustain them throughout their lives. It features a learning press agency, national awareness days and a national learning forum, as well as project partnerships, resources, events, research and advice.

Commonwealth of Learning
http://www.col.org
COL is an international organisation set up by Commonwealth governments in 1988. It exists to promote greater access to education and to improve its quality, using distance education techniques and communications technology.

Fig. 62. Cyber Bee, an educator's guide to using the internet. The web site includes some excellent web links covering most aspects of the school curriculum.

CyberBee (USA)
http://www.cyberbee.com/
From the home page of the CyberBee site, you can access a monthly newsletter designed to help educators navigate the internet. There are handy tips, updates on projects, and details of new sites.

DfEE – UK Lifelong Learning
http://www.lifelonglearning.co.uk/
You will find this an ever-changing site offering access to a variety of options. At the time of review there were links to basic skills, the single regeneration budget, demonstration outreach projects, lifelong learning partnerships, individual learning news online and other news. You can download information, use the search button and contact the DfEE.

EduForum
http://www.scholarstuff.com/
This site offers a meeting place for educators on the net.

European Council of International Schools (UK)
http://www.ecis.org/
ECIS is a membership organisation of international schools and institutions and individual members. You can link into membership, conferences, services, directories, jobs, chat, news, distance learning, resources, accreditation and consultancy.

International Interactive Communications Society (USA)
http://www.iics.org/
This site aims to promote interactive systems and the people who produce them. Its home page provides access to a job bank, membership of IICS, chapter links, a bookshelf and professional development.

Internet 2 (USA)
http://www.internet2.edu/
Internet2 is a major new US-led academic initiative, set up to develop advanced applications to meet academic needs throughout research, teaching and learning.

Learning for the 21st Century (UK)
http://www.lifelonglearning.co.uk/nagcell/index.htm
On this site you will find the first report of the National Advisory Group for Continuing Education and Lifelong Learning. You can also get a hard copy, and access their second report, *Creating Learning Cultures: Next Steps in Achieving the Learning Age* plus links to the UKLL and DfEE homepages.

Library of Congress (USA)
http://lcweb.loc.gov/global/internet/training.html
This site is a directory offering internet guides, individual online guides, courses, resources for internet trainers, tutorials and training information mainly provided by organisations outside the Library of Congress. It is part of the massive Library of Congress web site based in Washington.

National Grid for Learning (UK)
http://www.ngfl.gov.uk/
The NGFL is intended by the British government to become a national focal point for learning on the internet. From the home page you can link to schools, FE, HE, lifelong learning, career development, libraries, links,

government and agencies and learning resources. Clicking on other icons will take you to search, advice, feedback and discussion groups.

National Open College Network (UK)
http://www.nocn.ac.uk/
The NOCN offers a comprehensive accreditation service through a national framework of local open college networks. You can link into the its qualifications directory, open college networks, news, events, library, members' information area, and NOCN qualifications.

Project Happy Child (UK)
http://www.happychild.org.uk/schools/uk/england/index1.htm
A 'schools interchange' is being created here, so that schools, colleges and universities in the UK and the rest of the world can link up. The service is offered in English, French, Dutch, Italian, Portuguese and Spanish. There are additional links to educational resources, events, fundraising, software, appeals, sponsors, advertisers and contacts. The site contains handy links to school web sites in the UK arranged by county or local authority.

Route ICS (USA)
http://ics.soe.umich.edu/
This University of Michigan site provides an experiment in using the world wide web, not just for providing information, but also for creating communication links between students all over the world.

Rudolf Steiner Adult Education Centres (New Zealand)
http://www.ch.steiner.school.nz/adulted.html
There are links through this site to Rudolf Steiner centres in America, Sweden, New Zealand, Germany and Australia.

Schoolfinder (Canada)
http://www.schoolfinder.com/
SchoolFinder is a major Canadian education guide to universities, colleges and career colleges. You can customise your search of over 600 schools and find a detailed description of each one, including admission requirements, costs, programs and contact information.

TUC Education Online (UK)
http://www.education-online.co.uk/
You can link into Trade Union Congress conferences, a reference library and courses from here.

UK Further Education Higher Education & University Colleges (UK)
http://www.bham.ac.uk/webmaster/ukuwww.html
Produced by the University of Birmingham, this useful site offers links to the web sites of UK further and higher education institutions, including the universities, which are listed in aphabetical order and under their initial letter. There are also references to other web sites where you can search for information on further and higher education institutions.

School Info
universities
colleges
career colleges
graduate schools

Search
keyword search
custom search
quick search

Finances
free scholarships
student loans

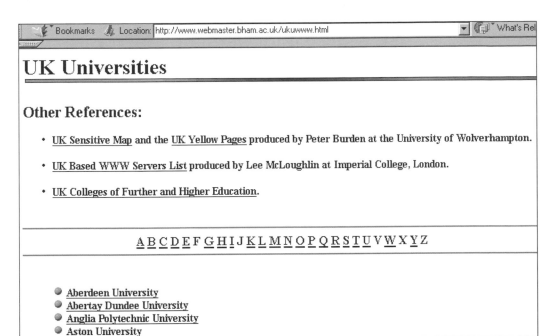

Fig. 63. UK Universities, useful web resource developed at the University of Birmingham.

UK Universities and Further Education Colleges (UK)
http://www.ja.net/janet-sites/university.html
The UK Academic & Research Network (JANET) offers a brief home page with the letters of the alphabet waiting for you to click on to them to access institution web sites. There are three clickable icons on the home page. One leads you to JANET, explaining how it links several hundred institutions, including universities and colleges, research council establishments and other organisations in the academic and research community.

University of Northumbria Education Liaison Service (UK)
http://www.northumbria.ac.uk/corporate/edliais.htm
This site offers a useful link between universities, schools and colleges across the UK and Eire, and guidance about entry requirements and study opportunities for potential applicants and their advisers.

US Department of Education (USA)
http://www.ed.gov/
Here you will find pages containing research, funding opportunities, student financial assistance, news, events, services, publications, departmental contacts, job openings, search, directories and links.

Web Ed (USA)
http://www.osc.edu/webED/links.html
This site is run by the Ohio Supercomputer Centre. The home page has a number of links into higher education, K-12 education, training and development. There is a news icon that leads to an extensive amount of current information on education and training. There are links to online courses,

articles, catalogues, campuses and virtual universities, conferences, forums and newsletters. Further links take you to free educational tools, courses for teaching online, and more.

Learning resources

British Education Index (UK)
http://www.ntu.ac.uk/lis/bids.htm
British Education Index is the UK's national database for every significant article on education and training. The articles are drawn from over 350 British and European English-language periodicals, dating back to 1976. It also holds the British Education Theses Index as a subfile. This is a subject guide to theses on educational topics accepted for higher degrees by universities in Great Britain and Ireland. You will need your ATHENS (BIDS) username and password to access this service.

Fig. 64. Learning on the Internet, a handy collection of links developed by YouthOrg UK, a virtual community for young people and professionals using the internet for learning. It is managed by Youth Clubs UK, the largest network of voluntary youth organisations in the UK.

BUBL WWW Subject Tree for Education (UK)
http://link.bubl.ac.uk/education/
This is a part of the authoritative BUBL academic gateway which leads to more than 500 educational resources worldwide.

Charles Sturt University WWW Virtual Library for Education (Australia)
http://www.csu.edu.au/education/library.html
This provides links to education resources by site, level, and country. It also offers handy links to the growing number of Usenet newsgroups devoted to education.

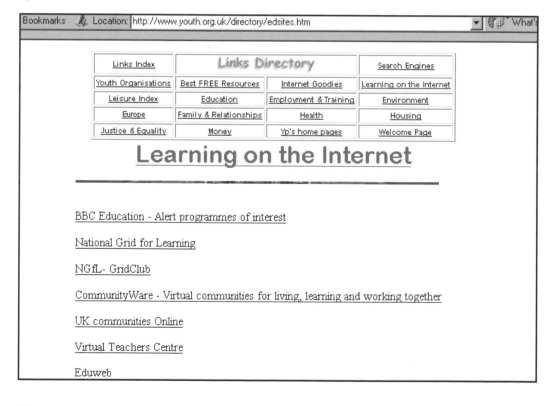

Education-line (UK)
http://www.leeds.ac.uk/educol/
This site offers access to various electronic texts in education and training. You can search for specific texts or submit texts.

Kalamazoo College Electronic Portfolios
http://www.kzoo.edu/ ~ pfolio/
Here you can find information about Kalamazoo's 'electronic portfolio'. This service helps students track their college experiences, and helps colleges incorporate experiential education into campus culture. Students review their electronic portfolios with their advisors at each course selection time, and with other mentors at various times during the year.

Learning on the Internet (UK)
http://www.youth.org.uk/directory/edsites.htm
This Youth Internet Project site helps youth workers and young people learn how to make effective use of the net. The benefits of membership include a web address, advice, opportunities for participation, links, e-publications and a free newsletter.

Success Learning Systems (USA)
http://www.SLSonline.com/
This site details the company's software kits for early learning, elementary, and college education, and its new titles, catalogue, and online ordering service. You can explore about 150 tutorials which are available over the internet, and choose a free demo. The courses are mainly concerned with developing computer and internet skills.

Yahoo! Education
http://dir.yahoo.com/education/index.html
This site has links to a vast range of resources, including electronic journals, online teaching and learning, databases, television and news. Yahoo! is the world's biggest and most used internet search engine and directory.

Media and broadcasting

BBC Learning Zone (UK)
http://www.bbc.co.uk/education/lzone/
This site supports BBC2's overnight record-and-play service. All kinds of subjects are on offer every night, from languages to technology, computing, the environment and links, appealing to all ages and interests.

Discovery Channel Online (USA)
http://www.discovery.com/
This site gives access to colourful and interesting learning opportunities such as feature stories, exhibitions, mind games, live cams and conversations, and links to shops, books, guides and search.

Education Unlimited (UK)
http://www.educationunlimited.co.uk/
From the home page, you can access web links for parents, teachers and

lecturers from the Guardian Unlimited Network with additional links to special reports, resources plus articles from Education Guardian.

Edutv (UK)
http://www.edutv.org/
This is the web site of the Educational TV Unit of the European Broadcasting Union. You can access programmes for sale, educational TV and web sites and recent educational unit presentations.

Professional development

National Association of Teachers in Further & Higher Education (UK)
http://www.natfhe.org.uk/index.htm
NATFHE is the trade union and professional association for lecturers, researchers and managers in further and higher education in England, Wales and Northern Ireland.

National Union of Teachers (UK)
http://www.teachers.org.uk/
This informative site is suitable for students, teachers, governors, parents and pupils.

News International (UK)
http://www.newsint.co.uk/
This site gives you access to the *Times Higher Education Supplement* and *Times Educational Supplement*. You can subscribe, find academic job vacancies, or advertise.

Professional Development for Adult Educators (Canada)
http://www.sentex.net/~skeogh/profdev.html
This Ontario-based site contains a useful collection of topical articles and discussions about teacher training, teaching tips, and teaching styles in adult education. There is also a handy link on the home page to educational discussion group listservers.

TADSA for Employers (UK)
http://www.national-training.co.uk/info/tadsa/employ.htm
TADSA is a training and development staff agency specialising in contract and temporary assignments and permanent employment for nationally accredited trainers. This site provides services for finding, selecting, interviewing and cross-checking references and qualifications for training staff including temporary assignments, self-employed contractors and employed staff.

Teaching and Training Vacancies & Jobsearch (UK)
http://www.namss.org.uk/jobs_teach.htm
This is an excellent site offering links to jobsearch guidance and resources, plus several links to current vacancies in US and UK, as well as links into various education and training resources.

Thematic Network of Teacher Education (Sweden)
http://tntee.umu.se/
TNTEE is funded by the European Commission, as part of the Socrates/Erasmus programme. Its main objective is to establish a flexible multi-lingual trans-national forum for the development of teacher education in Europe linking together as many universities and other institutions as possible. You can link into subnetworks, an archive, discussions, publications and other links. You can choose a language for this site.

Virtual Teacher Centre (UK)
http://www.vtc.ngfl.gov.uk/vtc/
This site features a virtual reception area, library, meeting room, classroom resources, school management and professional development. There is a search facility.

Fig. 65. The Virtual Teachers Centre is a government-backed web site of resources developed by the UK National Grid for Learning (NGfL).

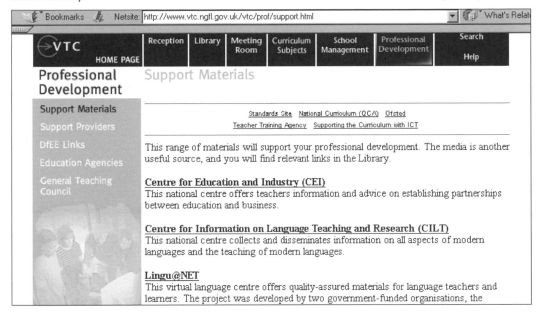

Young people and students

Britkid (UK)
http://www.britkid.org/
This is an excellent online game designed to educate British youngsters about racial issues and different cultures. Players learn about the lives of characters from varying ethnic backgrounds by 'hanging out' with them in the virtual town of Britchester. The project is funded with cash from Comic Relief.

Council Travel (USA)
http://www.counciltravel.com/
You can find travel information for students (and adults) covering air and rail on this site. Additional links take you to working and studying abroad, travel insurance, cool tours, hotels and hostels. Student Sign-Up gives

you email newsletters about travel opportunities, advance email announcements of special deals, discounts and promotions, a free copy of Student Travel's magazine and the chance to win some freebies.

Electronic Student Pages (UK)

http://www.studentpages.com/

This site is maintained by Student Solutions Ltd, a subsidiary of the careers publisher, Hobsons. On the home page, there are half a dozen clickable icons. One takes you to a 'virtual freshers' fair'. Another takes you to *Informer*, a nationwide listing of film times and reviews. You can also search the shops and services listings for details of Student Pages discount vouchers. The members icon enables you to become a VIP member, making you eligible for prizes and giveaways. The City Live area informs you about clubs, pubs and restaurants plus shopping and services for your town. You can keep in touch with the music scene via the Zine icon. Finally there's an icon which links you to the rest of the web. A link to Blackwell's online bookshop appears on the home page.

Kid Info (USA)

http://www.kidinfo.com/

There are four clear sites to follow: student, young children (colouring pages online), teacher (internet resources and web-integrated lesson plans), and parents (resources and lifestyle). There is a search function and a contact point.

Montessori (UK)

http://www.montessori.co.uk/index.htm

The Maria Montessori method of pre-school learning aims to 'allow children to grow naturally, to retain their individuality and develop their own, unique personality'. This site lists, among other things, Montessori equipment, seminars, software, furniture and teacher training establishments.

National Association for Managers of Student Services (UK)

http://www.namss.org.uk/

This is an organisation of managers of student services with members in institutions funded, wholly or in part, by the Further Education Funding Council, throughout the post-compulsory education sector. The site provides information and support for students and staff. There are two icons on the home page – one for students and one for staff. Both lead you to the same page that is split into two. The left-hand side is the Staff Pathway and the right-hand side is the Students' and Visitors' Pathway, each leading to further pages and links. Typical options for staff include New Deal & Welfare to Work and staff development and training. Typical options under students include accommodation, work experience and student unions. This site is 'Bobby Approved' (Bobby is a web-based tool that analyses web pages for their accessibility to people with disabilities).

Student Conservation Association (USA)

http://www.sca-inc.org/

The SCA allows you to serve the great outdoors while tapping into an inner personal landscape you may never have known existed. With hands-on service opportunities lasting up to a year, students as young as 16 can blaze a new trail of conservation service, experiential environmental education, career skills and leadership training.

Student Letter Exchange (USA)
http://www.pen-pal.com/
The Student Letter Exchange matches English-speaking pen pals with students aged 9 to 18 across the US and around the world. From the home page you can visit student pen pal registration, an adult pen pal directory, and contact points.

StudentsUK (UK)
http://www.studentuk.com/
From the home page you can click on news, clearing (plus a UCAS link), films, advice (on anything), soap (a student soap in instalments), travel, music, careers, politics and sport. There is a search button on the home page. You can register to join UniverCity to chat. From the home page you can send ecards, be part of an opinion poll and go online shopping for gear and gigs. Another click will take you to GraduBase, a searchable database of graduate employers. This facility will enable you to find contact information for graduate employers that fit your needs.

Student Unions, Student & Young People's Sites (UK)
http://www.namss.org.uk/student.htm
This site offers links to student unions, students' and young people's sites, youth work, NAMSS sites, careers and job search, study skills, finance, trade unions, work experience, online books to purchase, health, clearing sites and course information online.

Student World (UK)
http://www.student-world.com
This web site offers help, advice, chat, information, fun and online services for students, graduates and academic staff. There are several clickable icons on the home page, or you could use the search function. You can explore which institute to study with, investigate insurance, banking and finance options or look at resources and information related to computing. Other icons take you to news, media and research sites. You can go to the sport, leisure and travel site or spend money shopping online. There is an icon for culture, music and arts. You can also submit articles for the site.

StudentZone (UK)
http://www.studentzone.org.uk/
StudentZone offers services to further and higher education students and staff. You can click-on the above-left buttons for the noticeboard, comments, searching or help. Or you can click-onto a topic on the left-hand menu to find out what the sections are all about. The section covers areas such as academic, careers, news, travel, legal and finance, health, sport, life and the more cryptic 'ents' (entertainment) and 'bods' (organisations

which can be useful to know). Again from the home page, there's a noticeboard site which lists current and forthcoming student event information. You can email the StudentZone editorial team.

Teens Online (USA)
http://www.teens-online.com/chat.html
Visit this site for online chat, cyberpals, student homepages, a teen ezine, teen advice net, college chat and loads of other 'cool stuff'.

Fig. 66. UK Socrates-Erasmus. This network project allows students to become immersed in another culture, make new friends, obtain a working knowledge of another language, and develop skills contributing to employability.

UK Socrates-Erasmus (UK)
http://www.ukc.ac.uk/erasmus/erasmus/
From the home page, you can access information for students and universities about foreign study opportunities offered by the organisation in European countries, including answers to FAQs and regular newsletters.

Related chapters

Chapter 2 – School and college web sites
Chapter 3 – Higher education online
Chapter 4 – Vocational training web sites
Chapter 5 – Occupational training sites
Chapter 7 – Distance and online learning web sites
Chapter 10 – Your own education and training site

Related Internet Handbooks

The Internet for Students, David Holland (Internet Handbooks).
Where to Find It on the Internet, Kye Valongo (Internet Handbooks, 2nd edition).

10 Your own education & training site

In this chapter we will explore:

▶ *why have your own site?*

▶ *what do you need to start?*

▶ *skills of the online tutor*

▶ *the web as a tool for course delivery*

▶ *the profile of an online learner*

▶ *factors to consider in online learning*

▶ *developing online material*

▶ *managing learner interaction*

▶ *virtual classrooms*

▶ *web course development tools*

. . . .

Why have your own site?

There are three basic reasons for creating an education and training site:

1. To provide information to the general public. This could be pure information such as providing a network of school links. Or the site could be for commercial information, hooking the customer into contacting you for further information as a training consultancy might do.

2. To sell and support online courses.

3. To facilitate an internal learning network via an intranet (internal network). Schools, educational institutions and companies can all do this.

What do you need to start?

Hardware and software
In order to develop instruction for, and deliver it on, the web, you will need certain hardware and software configurations. So will your target learners. As the provider you will need a high-end computer with internet connectivity and an HTTP (hypertext transfer protocol) server software package. The developer of your web site and material is likely to want one or more of the HTML editors or tools. Finally the end-user will need at least a computer with a modem and internet connectivity software and a web browser. Below are some of the most commonly used tools:

Hardware
A minimum 486 or preferably a Pentium 200 mHz personal computer (PC) with at least 32mb of RAM (random access memory). It should have a hard disk of at least 1 gigabyte (1,000 megabytes), a CD-rom drive, and an internal or external modem running at not less than 28,800 bps (bits per second).

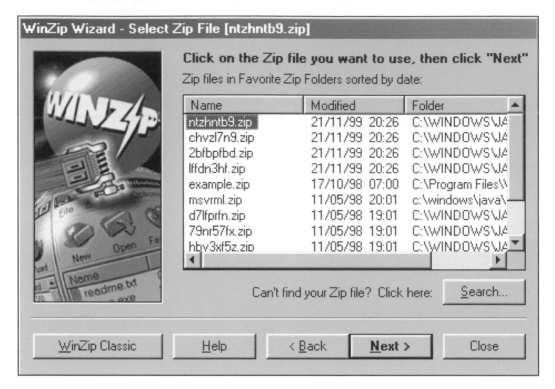

```
WinZip Wizard - Select Zip File [ntzhntb9.zip]

          Click on the Zip file you want to use, then click "Next"

          Zip files in Favorite Zip Folders sorted by date:

          Name              Modified          Folder
          ntzhntb9.zip      21/11/99 20:26    C:\WINDOWS\JA
          chvzl7n9.zip      21/11/99 20:26    C:\WINDOWS\JA
          2bfbpfbd.zip      21/11/99 20:26    C:\WINDOWS\JA
          lffdn3hf.zip      21/11/99 20:26    C:\WINDOWS\JA
          example.zip       17/10/98 07:00    C:\Program Files\\
          msvrml.zip        11/05/98 20:01    c:\windows\java\
          d7lfprfn.zip      11/05/98 19:01    C:\WINDOWS\JA
          79nr57fx.zip      11/05/98 19:01    C:\WINDOWS\JA
          hbv3xf5z.zip      11/05/98 19:01    C:\WINDOWS\JA

          Can't find your Zip file? Click here:     Search...

  WinZip Classic       Help        < Back      Next >        Close
```

Fig. 67. WinZip, some handy software for opening up and using compressed ('zipped') files such as software which you may download from the internet.

Software

1. A computer operating system (OS) – typically Windows 3.1, Windows 95 or Windows 98.

2. WinZip 6.2. Many of the useful programs that you can download from the internet are compressed to make them smaller and so quicker to download. Once they have been loaded onto your computer, WinZip expands them back to their original size so that they can start to do their job. You can download WinZip from: http://www.winzip.de/com

3. A web browser, so you can look at web pages. By far the two most popular are Internet Explorer 5 (http://www.microsoft.com/ie/download/) or Netscape Navigator 4 (http://live.netscape.com/comprod/mirror/client.download.html). These two browsers are almost always included on the free CD-roms on the covers of the monthly computer magazines.

4. A word processor. The very basic Notepad word processor should already be on your PC (try clicking Start, Programs, Accessories, Notepad). A far more powerful one is MicroSoft Word.

5. A graphics package such as PaintShop Pro which can be obtained direct from its authors at: http://www.mindworkshop.com/alchemy/gifcon.html.

6. You will also need dial-up account with an internet service provider. The best known ones in the UK include Freeserve, BT, America On-Line (AOL), CompuServe, Demon and Virgin. A useful list of UK service providers is available at:

   http://www.limitless.co.uk/inetuk/table-provider.html

7. Some file transfer (FTP) software, so you can transfer ('upload') your new web pages to your freespace or other web host location. The best known packages include WS.FTP (http://www.ipswitch.com), CuteFTP (http://www.globalscape.com), and VoyagerFTP (http://ftpvoyager.deerfield.com). Free evaluation versions should be available.

Fig. 68. When you have created your web pages, you need some basic software to upload them to your freespace or other web host. WS.FTP from Ipswitch.com does the job easily and quickly.

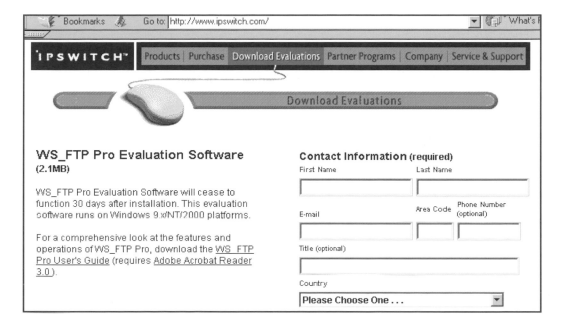

Editors
Editors are tools that help you create web documents without actually having to write the HTML tags. There are numerous editors for use on every platform. They fit into three basic types: stand-alone, converters, and template (or add-on). Stand-alone are applications which work, for the most part, independent of other applications. They usually include a text editor and ways to automatically add HTML tags to the text you are editing. Converters change text from some format to HTML. Templates and add-ons work within other programs, usually word processors, to allow you to create HTML-formatted documents within those applications. Editors, especially those that can convert already written materials, can speed the production of HTML documents.

Viewers and other helper applications
Most browsers are capable of displaying text and graphic images such as

GIFs (filename extension '.gif'). Many of them support JPEG images (file-name extension '.jpg'). A few offer limited support for audio and video. But most browsers have to use another program to handle file types which are not supported internally.

You can specify these viewers and helper applications in your own browser. They range from QuickTime and MPEG movie viewers to telnet and other internet applications. In order for the browser to activate these applications, users will also need to have them available on their computer. The applications vary from platform to platform. To begin with, it is better to keep things as simple as you can.

Skills of the online tutor

If you are considering developing skills as an online tutor, you will need the following:

1. Familiarity with hypertext markup language (HTML).

2. Familiarity with the creation, editing and saving of files, and transfer-ring ('uploading' or 'ftping') those files to a web site.

3. If creating audio or video files, or using graphics or Java programs on a web page, familiarity with these file formats and their incorporation into a web site.

4. Awareness of instructional design principles.

5. An understanding of the learners' goals, needs, preferences, and anxi-eties about learning and the content being explored.

6. Consideration of the variety of learning environments in terms of tech-nological resources and the physical environment surrounding the computer being used.

7. Awareness of learning purposes and/or objectives that take into ac-count personal and learning environment factors.

8. Examination of alternative technologies as teaching tools.

9. Ability to select technologies that are appropriate for the objectives or purposes based in the learners' needs, their learning environment and the content.

10. Monitoring and reinforcing the learning progress through course de-sign and opportunities for continual interaction throughout the experi-ence.

11. Provision of opportunities for learners to evaluate their progress and the learning experience.

The web as a tool for course delivery

Many tutors today believe that they must have a text to deliver a course. This is because print-based media have dominated our lives since child-

Bookmarks   Go to: http://webct.wiley.com   ▼   What's Rel

Welcome to the Wiley WebCT Course for Psychology: Mind, Brain & Culture, 2e. by Drew Westen

Course Content

This course contains the following:

STUDENT

- 3-5 Student Exercises per Chapter
- 10 Self-Quizzes by Chapter
- Web Links
- On-line Survival Guide
- In the News (Science News: updated bi-weekly)

INSTRUCTOR

- Test Bank
- PowerPoint Slides
- Lecture Outlines
- Compiling course content (syllabi)
- In the News (Science News: updated bi-weekly)

hood. The textbook has long been the basic tool of teaching. Why is hypertext different? The web is a new phenomenon, and web-based course materials just do not have the tradition that textbooks have. Is hypertext a less useful tool for instruction? Quite the contrary – hypertext is much *more* useful. It can link to almost any other document on the web – hundreds of millions of them – often in a matter of seconds.

One obstacle deters many tutors. They believe 'you have to be a computer programmer' to build web pages. Of course, you have to use a computer if you want to develop web pages, but it does *not* mean you to have to learn any programming. Most web processors can turn out web pages just as easily as word-processed documents.

Think of this technology as just another tool for delivering instruction. It should and probably will become another necessary tool for teaching. Do the tools of education and training have any bearing on design? Of course! All instruction is delivered through one medium or another. Even a traditional face-to-face course delivery can be thought of as being delivered through a 'spoken' medium. All media have their intrinsic advantages and disadvantages, and instruction should be designed accordingly.

Fig. 69. WebCT is one of the most popular and well-regarded software packages enabling tutors and colleges to deliver learning over the internet. It has 6 million student accounts in 147,000 courses at more than 1,350 colleges and universities in 55 countries (http://www.webct.com).

The profile of an online learner

(a) highly computer literate

(b) already using basic internet skills

(c) shows a willingness to take the risk of taking a class online

(d) demonstrates more thoughtfulness of questions

(e) older and more mature

(f) likely to be working full time

(g) increased motivation

Factors to consider in online learning

The following issues need to be addressed if you are considering developing an education or training site on the web:

1. quality of learning
2. interaction between learner and tutor
3. quality class participation
4. assessment of learning
5. test security
6. learner skill and equipment requirements
7. ranges of ages or life-stages of learners
8. educational and experiential background of learners
9. learners' previous experiences with technology
10. learners' access to the web

Benefits and dangers of new learning technologies

Where does assessment fit into learning technologies? If we're wired up for sound so to speak, to a screen, how is our learning monitored and assessed? Traditional learning is characterised by learner observation, product assessment, group discussion, individual presentation, and questioning or paper assessment. With technology-based learning, too, we need to ensure that assessment and monitoring of learning is taking place.

Computers can do this (CAA, computer-assisted assessment), but the human factor is needed, too. For example, some skills need to be observed in action, such as customer care. We might be able to gain an understanding of customer care via technology; and we can demonstrate this through technology. But we can only assess someone's skills in action with a troublesome customer by face-to-face assessment. There are several excellent online management courses – but again we need the human touch to provide a revolving platform for holistic learning.

We need a balanced strategy combining action learning, face-to-face interventions, and technology. The motivation to learn cannot be created, delivered or supported by technology alone. Learning needs to happen in an integrated way.

We need to consider how people like to learn. Not everyone is suited to sitting in front of a computer. Incorporating learning styles such as listening and reading, observing and imitating, doing and feedback into a learning programme, alongside learning technologies, needs to be observed. Some learners may lean more towards technology as being the best way for them. Others may need coaching or group training with a reduced technological content.

In the age of the internet, it would be wrong to depersonalise learning. After all, learning can happen anywhere and at anytime. The sharing of personal experience and the personal reassurance of a tutor/trainer or peer learner can improve learning. We can still have the personal touch with technology, but the contact is one step removed. Although technology can break down barriers, it can also be a barrier in itself – if used in isolation!

Key questions you might ask when considering learning technologies are:

1. How often do we need to update learning technologies? What is the cost?

2. How do we cover technical breakdown? What is the cost?

3. Do learning styles and practices in the training-room apply to new learning technologies?

4. Are new learning styles and activities emerging from the experience of new learning technologies?

5. How can learners judge the relevance of and exercise control over the direction of their learning, monitor their progress, set objectives and demonstrate their achievements?

6. What support systems can be put in place?

7. Is there a role for face-to-face contact with trainers and other learners?

8. How can interpersonal skills be developed?

Positive factors in favour of new learning technologies
▶ mobile locations

▶ learners can participate at times to suit them

▶ there is the potential for international learning

▶ information can be speedily transferred

▶ there is increased networking potential internally and externally

▶ learning the core skills leads to the organic growth of further technical skills

▶ technology can extend the learner's progress beyond course boundaries into self-directed learning

Your own education & training site ....

Fig. 70. Demonstration example of a Psychology course produced by John Wiley & Sons, using the WebCT software package in figure 69.

Developing online material

Key steps for planning your online learning

1. Create an overall 'road map' for your course.
2. Identify learning objectives and goals.
3. Identify the content you will cover.
4. Plan how to communicate assignments and schedule any changes.
5. Identify the approaches you will use.
6. Identify how interaction will be incorporated.
7. Identify the materials learners will need to successfully complete the course.
8. Identify plans for grading and testing.
9. Identify how you would like learners to contact you.
10. Plan and provide an online tutorial or sample lesson.

Special considerations for distance education courses

(a) develop a homepage to help identify your course to learners
(b) inform learners in advance about the hardware and software they will need
(c) provide basic internet and web information for novice distance education learners
(d) provide information about distance learner support services

(e) develop instructional content that will 'stand alone' for distant learners

(f) keep file sizes small for modem use

Five steps to designing a basic web page

1. Decide on the text, pictures and graphics you want in your page.

2. Use a text editor such as Notepad to write the text. If you browse with Netscape Navigator, you will find a useful Page Composer that lets you write web pages just as if you were word processing. You could use HTML (hypertext markup language) to write your page. A good place to start is The HTML Writers Guild which offers advice and software (http://www.hwg.org). Some well-known HTML editors include Microsoft FrontPage, and HotDog (http://www.sausage.com). You could turn your Word for Windows into a good HTML package by bolting on an authoring tool such as Microsoft Internet Assistant.

3. Edit and format the graphics you want.

4. Preview your web pages using a graphical browser (e.g. Internet Explorer or Netscape Navigator).

5. Upload your web pages to a server (host computer) using your dial-up account with an internet service provider.

Converting existing documents
Next time you are word processing, take a closer look at the 'File' menu. Many word processors like Microsoft Word 97 allow you to save existing documents as web pages (HTML). That makes them not just word processors but 'web processors.' It could hardly be easier.

Eleven tips for good web design
1. Keep it interactive.

2. Keep it relevant.

3. Keep promoting it.

4. Keep it organised.

5. Keep it fast.

6. Keep it tidy.

7. Keep it linked.

8. Keep your focus.

9. Keep it interesting.

10 Keep changing it.

11. Keep giving away information.

Your own education & training site ....

In the traditional classroom, a pleasing voice, occasional jokes, dramatic gestures, and interspersed questions can help to enliven a long lecture. When putting learning material on the web – even if the workstation supports colour graphics and sound – long segments of lecture-type materials are boring. To maintain interest, the tutor should use written language in a skilful way (including humour and metaphor), orchestrate active participation by the learners, and stimulate collaborative assignments requiring both social and task-oriented activities. Do not try to deliver a long 'lecture' in written format. Instead, deliver small segments accompanied with opportunities for participation. Use print or pre-recorded materials for purely 'lecture' materials.

One consideration in web course design is that the types of interactions must be taken into account when designing course activities. Moore and Kearsley (1996) describe three types of interactions that can take place in an online environment:

(a) Learner-content interaction has occurred since the invention of text-based materials. In this type of interaction, learners are expected to construct their own knowledge from the materials provided. Study guides supplement this type of interaction, and provide the foundation on which learners can build their knowledge.

(b) Learner-tutor interaction is regarded by many as pre-eminent. In addition to presenting subject matter, tutors motivate learners, provide guidance, and demonstrate procedures. Their main role is to facilitate learning. This two-way interaction can benefit both learners and tutors.

(c) Learner-learner interaction often arises spontaneously when challenged learners turn to their peers for help. But this type of interaction can and should be encouraged in all learners. Peer teaching and learning is a powerful instrument at any level.

Each interaction is supported by different technologies. Selecting and managing these technologies to best facilitate appropriate interactions for a particular course and group of learners is the art of web course development.

With HTML it is easy to simply start putting information together and putting it on the web. But in itself this has little to do with creating instruction. Instruction is the deliberate organisation and presentation of information with the goal of promoting specific learning. When designing WBI it is critical to keep the instructional aspects uppermost in mind. The snazziest web site can still be useless at guiding a learner towards a stated goal if it is not created with sound instructional technique in mind.

Managing learner interaction

How tutors approach interaction with learners enrolled online may depend on how much value is placed on interaction for achieving the purposes of the course. Unless the course design includes opportunities for synchronous meetings, there are several things to consider about online interaction as the course progresses:

1. Learners will be interacting with the course at all times of the day.
2. Learners will be interacting with the tutor (via email or other means) at all times of the day.
3. Online tutors will find it useful to establish guidelines for communications as soon as the course begins.
4. Learners are not going to attend the next class meeting to hear announcements.
5. Learners probably do not see themselves as interrupting, or taking time away from other learners, when interacting with the tutor by email. They can also reflect before putting questions to the tutor.
6. More opportunities are available for providing useful feedback to learners, but those opportunities bring additional time management, privacy, and integrity concerns.
7. Online learners will need much the same support systems and resources that traditional learners need, but they may need to access them in different ways.

Probably the biggest influence on whether learners prefer online delivery to traditional methods is their interaction with tutors and/or other learners. This interaction is not always easy to organise, but if you can cajole the learners into a collaborative approach, they will productively share ideas with each other in a way that is seldom seen in a traditional classroom.

Virtual classrooms (VC)

A 'virtual classroom' is not always the proper mode for all tutors or all learners. Tutors need to feel comfortable with computers and with writing. A minimum of about ten active participants seems to be necessary to establish and maintain a lively interchange. In order to succeed, learners must have convenient access to a computer and modem, reasonable reading and writing skills, and the time, motivation, and self-discipline to participate regularly. Learners lacking the necessary basic skills and self-discipline may do better on a traditional course.

Whether or not the VC mode is 'better' also depends crucially on how far the tutor can develop a co-operative and collaborative learning group. New skills are needed to teach in this new way. Probably the single most important factor in producing good results is timely and 'personal' responses by tutors to the questions and contributions of learners online.

Web course development tools

The following sites offer support for those wishing to design and develop online learning environments. The web course development packages offer a variety of integrated tools to delivery web based instruction. The features of these different courseware packages vary, but each allows for the creation and organisation of a web site. In addition they facilitate communication and collaboration through basic tools like the course bulletin board, chat, and email. Other features may include online quizzing, grade management, statistics generation, and learner tracking.

CaMILE (USA)
http://www.cc.gatech.edu/gvu/edtech/CaMILE.html
CaMILE stands for Collaborative and Multimedia Interactive Learning Environment, a web-based tool for use by students designed to encourage learning, developed at the College of Computing, Georgia Institute of Technology. It prompts students to identify the kind of notes they are contributing to a collaboration and suggests things to say in them. The goal is to encourage metacognition.

Campus America: 'The Learning Manager' (USA)
http://www.campus.com/
Campus America has 20-year track record in information technology for education. It offers tools for curriculum development, instructional design, and course delivery. It is useful in traditional training or virtual learning environments using PC and client/server for distance learning, interactive multimedia, computer managed learning, computer aided instruction, competency-based training, open learning, flexible delivery and knowledge production.

Centra Software: Symposium (USA)
http://www.centra.com
Centra provides state-of-the-art education and training programs, including Symposium. It aims to help presenters, educators, curriculum developers, content developers, instructional designers, tutors, systems administrators, and other business professionals in using its material. It offers Symposium-delivered sessions, tutor-led classroom training, education consulting, content developer program, and some certification programs. It runs modules on designing sessions, creating content, converting existing content, using Symposium Course Builder, best practices for presenters and leaders, holding effective Symposium meetings, and other topics.

Centre for Development of Teaching & Learning (Singapore)
http://www.cdtl.nus.sg/
The centre provides centralised training and support, promoting the development information technology for teaching/learning, helping in the production of media for teaching, and in Singapore University's development programme. It runs online computer skills courses on Microsoft FrontPage 98, PowerPoint 97, and Creating Web Pages for Beginners.

Centre for Knowledge Communication (USA)
http://www.cs.umass.edu/~ckc/
CKC is a research group in computer science at the University of Massachusetts, Amherst. It investigates the design and use of digital technology for learning and teaching. It researches and develops develop teaching systems which can work with a variety of learners, in a variety of domains, and with multiple tutoring strategies. Its training and instructional systems

provide online practice, synthesis, problem-solving and group activities. It deals also with task analysis, representation and control of knowledge, and the identification of tutoring rules and strategies.

Cinecom Corporation (USA)
http://www.cinecom.com/
This Virginia company specialises in video conferencing and internet/intranet connectivity. It supplies multimedia delivery systems for virtual classroom environments, software for virtual education, and corporate training. It produces user applications for virtual education (distance learning), a virtual help desk, online tutoring, corporate training, and virtual meetings or conferences. Its Virtual Educator delivers a complete distance-learning solution for use over local or wider area networks, and the internet. It consists of a tutor-controlled learning environment with web-based classes, multipoint video and audio, tutor-led web discussions, shared whiteboard and other features.

Class Net (USA)
http://classnet.cc.iastate.edu/
Class Net is designed to help manage and deliver instruction on the web. Classes can be created, assignments can be designed, administered and graded, and learners and tutors can communicate.

Class Point (USA)
http://www.wpine.com/cp
From White Pine Software you can access a videoconferencing server for classroom use. White Pine's new ClassPoint allows a teacher to see lear-

Fig. 71. You can use ClassNet to create classes, create and manage assignments, and communicate with students via email, chat and newsgroups.

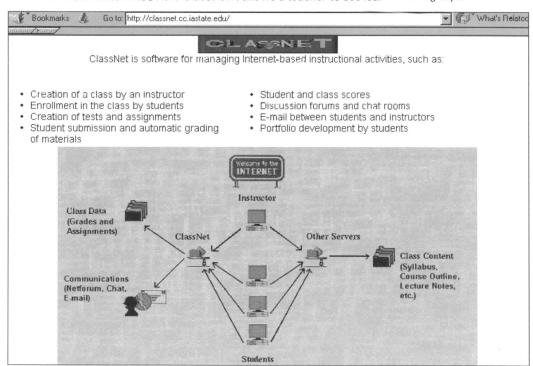

ners, to show them slides, watch them raise their hand (when they click a button), and take each off their web browsers on a tour.

Darryl Sink (USA)
http://www.dsink.com/
Darryl Sink has developed learning tools to supplement its range of workshops, and act as standalone products, including its course development software, CourseWriter 2.0. From the home page, you can link into its various instructional design products.

Designing Training for the Internet (UK)
http://www-iet.open.ac.uk/Courses/DTI/
'Designing training for the internet' has been written for training departments wanting to develop online training for their own organisation. It aims to help staff acquire the skills needed to design and deliver learning modules over the internet to technical and supervisory staff. It focuses on the web as a medium for distance learning, and includes the study of appropriate learner support and tutorial services using commuter-mediated communication. The course was produced at the Open University's Institute of Educational Technology.

Digital Think (USA)
http://www.digitalthink.com
Located in San Francisco, Digital Think designs, develops and deploys e-learning solutions. From its home page you can visit the pressroom, subscribe for news by email, look at IT courses and explore its corporate e-learning solutions. Other icons lead you to contacts, careers and support.

Ed Tech Tools (USA)
http://motted.hawaii.edu/
This is a co-operative project developed at the University of Hawaii, as a free online service for educators. Among the online programs it offers are the QuizCenter Online Service. Without any knowledge of HTML you can easily create internet-based quizzes for distance learning and online lesson plans. The site offers a working demonstration of QuizServer. The program is available for licensed installation on Windows and UNIX systems.

FirstClass Software (USA)
http://www.softarc.com
The FirstClass system from Centrinity is based on a client/server scheme. The server runs on both Macintosh and Windows NT systems, and is easy to install and configure. As well as letting users access the server over the internet, direct access is possible via a modem. Case study: the University of Maine uses FirstClass products to create an integrated, collaborative environment for its students and faculty. There are usually over 600 concurrent users on a single server.

FLAX (UK)

http://www.cms.dmu.ac.uk/coursebook/flax/

Flax helps you create interactive web pages and to collate materials you have created along with other resources on the web. From the home page you can see examples, look at course books, downloads, and get onto a mailing list.

Fig. 72. Flax Interactive Courseware is a British product. Its main intention is to support the creation of course books which are tutorials.

Hyper Studio (USA)

http://www.hyperstudio.com/

Hyper Studio is a multimedia authoring tool that lets you easily communicate and deliver your ideas on diskette, CD-rom or over the internet. You can use it to access data on the internet, create and edit QuickTime and AVI movies, and manage built-in image capture with AV Macs and/or digital cameras. It offers Mac/Windows/web project compatibility, wide file types compatibility for graphics, and sound.

HyperWave (USA)

http://www.hyperwave.com

HyperWave offers an approach based on document organisation and delivery over the internet. 'The Hyperwave Information Portal provides a desktop environment where end-users can go to gather information, share knowledge, and collaborate with others.'

In Depth Learning Web (USA)

http://www.indepthl.com/

In Depth provides tool for online learning systems and CBT, authorware, Director, Macromedia consulting, computer workshops for teachers, 3D illustration, web publishing, databases, and programming. It bases its curricula on goal-based scenarios and integrated thematic instruction models. The curriculum can be delivered on the web, on CD-rom, or as traditional print media.

Informedia (UK)
http://www.informedia.co.uk/learnonline.htm
Based in Kingston -upon- Hull, Informedia designs and implements interactive training materials for delivery across the internet or corporate intranets, using Asymetrix software. This includes the design of the user interface for interactive course delivery, systems for candidate-tracking and online course assessment, and the hosting of online learning materials and course delivery systems.

Instructional Design Solutions (USA)
http://www.idstraining.com/
IDS develops online training and courseware for delivery through a tutor, performance support system, or intranet. It specialises in creating training for customer service call centre operations.

Instructional Systems (USA)
http://www.isinj.com/
ISI offers college developmental courses in reading, maths, and writing. They take the form of computerised educational programs for schools, community colleges, social service training centres, and job training facilities.

Lecture Web (Australia)
http://lectureweb.turnaround.com.au/
Lecture Web from Tasmania enables the publishing of documents for a distributed online teaching environment. It allows for the central creation of any number of courses. Each one can be administered individually, with the teacher being responsible for updating content, or this responsibility can be delegated to someone else. You can run student mailing lists, and keep the individual look and feel of your sites by using custom templates.

Lotus Learning Space (USA)
http://www.lotus.com/
You can access powerful software through this site that has strong collaboration features, plus messaging and course administration tools.

Microsoft Exchange Server (USA)
http://www.microsoft.com/exchange/
Exchange Server is designed to support a large-scale collaboration environment. It integrates on a single platform all the communications and information-sharing capabilities needed to conduct asynchronous learning. It embraces virtually all internet standards and offers a foundation for rich, secure messaging and collaboration.

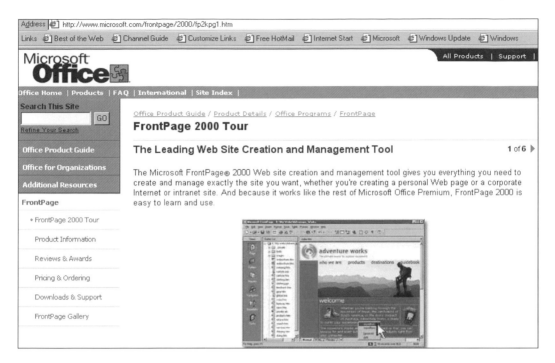

Microsoft FrontPage (USA)
http://www.microsoft.com/frontpage/
With this popular and inexpensive software (FrontPage 2000) you can
create and web-publish a wide variety of course content, lesson plans,
and class presentations which you have already created using MS Office
(Word, Access, Excel, Powerpoint). The software, which requires no
knowledge of HTML, allows you to create structured learner activities
online. You can develop assignments, conduct exams, and add a discussion group.

Microsoft in Higher Education (USA)
http://www.microsoft.com/education/hed/
Many people and organisations are already using the desktop productivity applications as the first step in creating course content. This web site
takes you through the next steps: putting course materials online, and
creating a rich infrastructure for learning and collaboration.

New Tools for Teaching (USA)
http://ccat.sas.upenn.edu/teachdemo
The home page leads to others that introduce, describe, and exemplify
new internet-based resources for teaching that are already available.
There are clickable icons to take you to the library, news groups, web
tools, a virtual classroom and contact point.

Online Delivery Applications (Canada)
http://www.ctt.bc.ca/landonline/index.html
This site is designed to help educators evaluate and choose the right

Fig. 73. MicroSoft
FrontPage is a popular
web authoring package,
designed to work
seamlessly with other
MicroSoft products such
as the Office suite. Its web
site provides an online
tour explaining how to use
the package effectively.

online delivery software. It describes and compares the best applications in use in Canada. The project is a collaborative venture by the British Columbia Standing Committee on Educational Technology and other educational bodies.

Quest (USA)
http://www.allencomm.com/
This site provides a range of tools and services for successful multimedia development: pre-authoring, instructional design, multimedia authoring, training delivery, management, custom courseware solutions, and consulting. Clicking other links will take you to solutions including TNA, events, the Academy of Multimedia, and custom courseware development. There is a download option as well as a search facility and contact icon.

QuestWriter (USA)
http://www.peak.org/qw
This site is based at Oregon State University. QuestWriter is a set of tools which make it possible to teach a course entirely online. It allows the creation of quizzes and other activities which students can do using the world wide web. The results are automatically recorded and entered into a gradebook. It automatically groups students into discussion groups, and provides a structured forum for pursuing a discussion topic.

Fig. 74. QuestWriter supports online course materials. PEAK, also offered on the home page, supports online education.

Question Mark (UK)
http://www.qmark.com/
Since being set up ten years ago, London-based Question Mark has become a leader in computerised assessment software. Its products are

easy to use and highly secure, making it suitable for almost any type of organisation or business. It is used by organisations in over 50 countries. Major corporations, universities, schools, and governments use it to administer all kinds of tests, assessments and surveys. The site can be viewed in several different languages.

Socrates Program (USA)
http://www.esocrates.com/
This is more of a 'service' than a tool. You can create web pages for your course with their templates and they will post them on their server. It creates an 'electronic syllabus' for your courses. It offers two types of teaching web sites: Passport and Forum. These are designed with all online teaching tools, interactivity tools, and educational resources of the web embedded in them. 'You can launch online courses in a day.'

ToolBook (USA)
http://www.asymetrix.com/
Through this site, you can access online IT and sales training and authoring tools. Clicking on various icons will take you to their consultancy service, technical support, system integration, guidance on setting up online training, and custom development. There is a search facility.

Virtual Learning (Canada)
http://www.virtuallearning.net/
This firm specialises in the application of new learning and marketing strategies to the healthcare industries. It develops, maintains and supports a comprehensive line of software to support learning and education, e-marketing, change management, and consulting practices. Programs are designed to provide ongoing feedback to participants as well as outcomes or performance measures for the program sponsor.

WebCT (Canada)
http://www.webct.com/
This well-known site originally developed at the University of British Columbia gives you access to a widely used tool for creating courseware on the internet. WebCT is an easy-to-use environment for creating sophisticated web-based courses that are otherwise beyond the ability of the non-computer programmer. The system includes various attractively designed templates which you can combine as needed.

WebMentor (USA)
http://www.avilar.com
This Maryland site sells a software product for web-based education and distance learning. The links on the home page take you into authoring, the product, demo courses, support, collaboration, the management team, pricing, contact points and press releases. Each course can be customised for a diverse student population using attributes embedded in the course material. Animation, voice and video can be included.

Your own education & training site ....

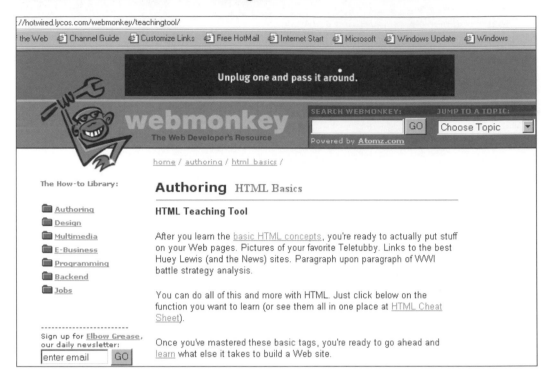

Fig. 75. Web Monkey is one of the best-known web sites dedicated to web authoring tools – what they are, and how to use them. If you are planning to create your own web pages, this site is a must.

Web Monkey: Teaching Tool (USA)
http://www.hotwired.com/webmonkey/teachingtool/
This is a very popular and widely used site for web development. From the home page you can learn step-by-step about web authoring, design, multimedia, e-business, programming and backend (all with sub topics). The information is all very breezily and clearly presented. There is a button for jobs and contacts, and you can sign up for *Elbow Grease*, a daily email newsletter. Learning some new skills here could change your life.

Internet Handbooks of related interest

Creating a Home Page on the Internet, Richard Cochrane (Internet Handbooks).
Building a Web Site on the Internet, Brendan Murphy (Internet Handbooks).
Getting Started on the Internet, Kye Valongo (Internet Handbooks).

Visit the free Internet HelpZone at
www.internet-handbooks.co.uk
Helping you master the internet

---

access provider – The company that provides you with access to the internet. This may be an independent provider or a large international organisation such as AOL or CompuServe. See also internet service provider.

ActiveX – A programming language that allows effects such as animations, games and other interactive features to be included a web page.

Adobe Acrobat – A type of software required for reading PDF files ('portable document format'). You may need to have Adobe Acrobat Reader when downloading large text files from the internet, such as lengthy reports or chapters from books. If your computer lacks it, the web page will prompt you, and usually offer you an immediate download of the free version.

address book – A directory in a web browser where you can store people's email addresses. This saves having to type them out each time you want to email someone. You just click on an address whenever you want it.

AltaVista – One of the half dozen most popular internet search engines. Just type in a few key words to find what you want on the internet: http://www.altavista.com

AOL – America OnLine, the world's biggest internet service provider, with more than 20 million subscribers, and now merged with Time Warner. Because it has masses of content of its own – quite aside from the wider internet – it is sometimes referred to as an 'online' service provider rather than internet service provider. It has given away vast numbers of free CDs with the popular computer magazines to build its customer base.

applet – An application programmed in Java that is designed to run only on a web browser. Applets cannot read or write data onto your computer, only from the domain in which they are served from. When a web page using an applet is accessed, the browser will download it and run it on your computer. See also **Java.**

application – Any program, such as a word processor or spreadsheet program, designed for use on your computer.

ARPANET – Advanced Research Projects Agency Network, an early form of the internet.

ASCII – American Standard Code for Information Interchange. It is a simple text file format that can be accessed by most word processors and text editors. It is a universal file type for passing textual information across the internet.

Ask Jeeves – A popular internet search engine. Rather than just typing in a few key words for your search, you can type in a whole question or instruction, such as 'Find me everything about online investment.' It draws on a database of millions of questions and answers, and works best with fairly general questions.

ASP – Active Server Page, a filename extension for a type of web page.

attachment – A file sent with an email message. The attached file can be anything from a word-processed document to a database, spreadsheet, graphic, or even a sound or video file. For example you could email someone birthday greetings, and attach a sound track or video clip.

Authenticode – Authenticode is a system where ActiveX controls can be authenticated in some way, usually by a certificate.

avatar – A cartoon or image used to represent someone on screen while taking part in internet chat.

backup – A second copy of a file or a set of files. Backing up data is essential if there is any risk of data loss.

Glossary of internet terms ....

bandwidth – The width of the electronic highway that gives you access to the internet. The higher the bandwidth, the wider this highway, and the faster the traffic can flow.

banner ad – This is a band of text and graphics, usually situated at the top of a web page. It acts like a title, telling the user what the content of the page is about. It invites the visitor to click on it to visit that site. Banner advertising has become big business.

baud rate – The data transmission speed in a modem, measured in bps (bits per second).

BBS – Bulletin board service. A facility to read and to post public messages on a particular web site.

binary numbers – The numbering system used by computers. It only uses 1s and 0s to represent numbers. Decimal numbers are based on the number 10. You can count from nought to nine. When you count higher than nine, the nine is replaced with a 10. Binary numbers are based on the number 2: each place can only have the value of 1 or 0. You can count from nought to one.

Blue Ribbon Campaign – A widely supported campaign supporting free speech and opposing moves to censor the internet by all kinds of elected and unelected bodies.

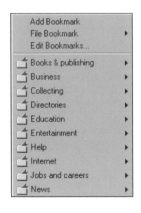

bookmark – A file of URLs of your favourite internet sites. Bookmarks are very easily created by bookmarking (mouse-clicking) any internet page you like the look of. If you are an avid user, you could soon end up with hundreds of them! In the Internet Explorer browser and AOL they are called 'favourites'.

boolean search – A search in which you type in words such as AND and OR to refine your search. Such words are called 'Boolean operators'. The concept is named after George Boole, a nineteenth-century English mathematician.

bot – Short for robot. It is used to refer to a program that will perform a task on the internet, such as carrying out a search.

browser – Your browser is your window to the internet, and will normally supplied by your internet service provider when you first sign up. It is the program that you use to access the world wide web, and manage your personal communications and privacy when online. By far the two most popular browsers are Netscape Communicator and its dominant rival Microsoft Internet Explorer. You can easily swap. Both can be downloaded free from their web sites and are found on the CD roms stuck to the computer magazines. It won't make much difference which one you use – they both do much the same thing. Opera, at http://www.opera.com is a great alternative that improves security, is faster and more efficient.

bug – A weakness in a program or a computer system.

bulletin board – A type of computer-based news service that provides an email service and a file archive.

cache – A file storage area on a computer. Your web browser will normally cache (copy to your hard drive) each web page you visit. When you revisit that page on the web, you may in fact be looking at the page originally cached on your computer. To be sure you are viewing the current page, press **reload** – or **refresh** – on your browser toolbar. You can empty your cache from time to time, and the computer will do so automatically whenever the cache is full. In Internet Explorer, pages are saved in the Windows folder, Temporary Internet Files. In Netscape they are saved in a folder called 'cache'.

certificate – A computer file that securely identifies a person or organisation on the internet.

CGI (common gateway interface) – This defines how the web server should pass information to the program, such as what it's being asked to do, what objects it should work with, any inputs, and so on. It is the same for all web servers.

channel (chat) – Place where you can chat with other internet chatters. The name of a chat channel is prefixed with a hash mark, #.

click through – This is when someone clicks on a banner ad or other link, for example, and is moved from that page to the advertiser's web site.

client – This is the term given to the program that you use to access the internet. For example your web browser is a web client, and your email program is an email client.

community – The internet is often described as a net community. This refers to the fact that many people like the feeling of belonging to a group of like-minded individuals. Many big web sites have been developed along these lines, such as GeoCities which is divided into special-interest 'neighbour-hoods', or America OnLine which is strong on member services.

compression – Computer files can be electronically compressed, so that they can be uploaded or downloaded more quickly across the internet, saving time and money. If an image file is compressed too much, there may be a loss of quality. To read them, you uncompress – 'unzip' – them.

content – Articles, columns, sales messages, images, and the text of your web site.

content services – Web sites dedicated to a particular subject.

cookie – A cookie is a small code that the server asks your browser to keep until it asks for it. If it sends it with the first page and asks for it back before each other page, they can follow you around the site, even if you switch your computer off in between.

cracker – Someone who breaks into computer systems with the intention of causing some kind of damage or abusing the system in some way.

crash – What happens when a computer program malfunctions. The operating system of your PC may perform incorrectly or come to a complete stop ('freeze'), forcing you to shut down and restart.

cross-posting – Posting an identical message in several different newgroups at the same time.

cybercash – This is a trademark, but is also often used as a broad term to de-scribe the use of small payments made over the internet using a new form of electronic account that is loaded up with cash. You can send this money to the companies offering such cash facilities by cheque, or by credit card. Some internet companies offering travel-related items can accept electronic cash of this kind.

cyberspace – Popular term for the intangible 'place' where you go to surf – the ethereal and borderless world of computers and telecommunications on the internet.

cypherpunk – From the cypherpunk mailing list charter: 'Cypherpunks assume privacy is a good thing and wish there were more of it. Cypherpunks ac-knowledge that those who want privacy must create it for themselves and not expect governments, corporations, or other large, faceless organisations to grant them privacy out of beneficence. Cypherpunks know that people have been creating their own privacy for centuries with whispers, envel-opes, closed doors, and couriers. Cypherpunks do not seek to prevent other people from speaking about their experiences or their opinions.'

cypherpunk remailer – Cypherpunk remailers strip headers from the mes-sages and add new ones.

data – hInformation. Data can exist in many forms such as numbers in a spread-sheet, text in a document, or as binary numbers stored in a computer's mem-ory.

Dial-Up Networking

dial up account – This allows you to connect your computer to your internet provider's computer remotely.

digital – Based on the two binary digits, 1 and 0. The operation of all computers is based on this amazingly simple concept. All forms of information are capable of being digitalised – numbers, words, and even sounds and images – and then transmitted over the internet.

directory – On a PC, a folder containing your files.

DNS – Domain name server.

domain name – A name that identifies an IP address. It identifies to the computers on the rest of the internet where to access particular information. Each domain has a name. For someone@somewhere.co.uk, 'somewhere' is the domain name. The domain name for Internet Handbooks for instance is: www.internet-handbooks.co.uk

download – 'Downloading' means copying a file from one computer on the internet to your own computer. You do this by clicking on a button that links you to the appropriate file. Downloading is an automatic process, except you have to click 'yes' to accept the download and give it a file name. You can download any type of file – text, graphics, sound, spreadsheet, computer programs, and so on.

ebusiness – The broad concept of doing business to business, and business to consumer sales, over the internet.

ecash – short for electronic cash. See cybercash.

ecommerce – The various means and techniques of transacting business online.

email – Electronic mail, any message or file you send from your computer to another computer using your 'email client' program (such as Netscape Messenger or Microsoft Outlook).

email address – The unique address given to you by your ISP. It can be used by others using the internet to send email messages to you. An example of a standard email address is:

mybusiness@aol.com

email bomb – An attack by email where you are sent hundreds or thousands of email messages in a very short period. This attack often prevents you receiving genuine email messages.

emoticons – Popular symbols used to express emotions in email, for example the well-known smiley   :-) which means 'I'm smiling!' Emoticons are not normally appropriate for business communications.

encryption – The scrambling of information to make it unreadable without a key or password. Email and any other data can now be encrypted using PGP and other freely available programs. Modern encryption has become so powerful that to all intents and purposes it is uncrackable. Law enforcers worldwide are pressing their governments for access to people's and organisation's passwords and security keys. Would you be willing to hand over yours?

Excite – A popular internet directory and search engine used to find pages relating to specific keywords which you enter. See also Yahoo!.

ezines – The term for magazines and newsletters published on the internet.

FAQ – Frequently asked questions. You will see 'FAQ' everywhere you go on the internet. If you are ever doubtful about anything check the FAQ page, if the site has one, and you should find the answers to your queries.

favorites – The rather coy term for **bookmarks** – used by Internet Explorer, and by America Online. Maintaining a list of 'favourites' is designed to make returning to a site easier.

file – A file is any body of data such as a wordprocessed document, a spreadsheet, a database file, a graphics or video file, sound file, or computer program.

filtering software – Software loaded onto a computer to prevent access by someone to unwelcome content on the internet, notably porn. The well-known 'parental controls' include CyberSitter, CyberPatrol, SurfWatch and

browser software available for surfing the internet. An excellent browser, Netscape has suffered in the wake of Internet Explorer, mainly because of the success of Microsoft in getting the latter pre-loaded on most new PCs. Netscape Communicator comes complete with email, newsgroups, address book and bookmarks, plus a web page composer, and you can adjust its settings in all sorts of useful ways. Netscape was taken over by American Online for $4 billion.

nettie – Slang term for someone who likes to spend a lot of time on the internet.

newbie – Popular term for a new member of a newsgroup or mailing list.

newsgroup – A Usenet discussion group. Each newsgroup is a collection of messages, usually unedited and not checked by anyone ('unmoderated'). Messages can be placed within the newsgroup by anyone including you. It is rather like reading and sending public emails. The ever-growing news-groups have been around for much longer than the world wide web, and are an endless source of information, gossip, news, entertainment, sex, pol-itics, resources and ideas. The 80,000-plus newsgroups are collectively re-ferred to as Usenet, and millions of people use it every day.

news reader – A type of software that enables you to search, read, post and manage messages in a newsgroup. It will normally be supplied by your inter-net service provider when you first sign up, or preloaded on your new com-puter. The best known are Microsoft Outlook, and Netscape Messenger.

news server – A remote computer (e.g. your internet service provider) that enables you to access the newsgroups on Usenet. If you cannot get some or any newsgroups from your existing news server, use your favourite search engine to search for 'open news servers' – there are lots of them freely avail-able. When you have found one you like, add it to your news reader by click-ing on its name. The first time you do this, it may take 10 to 20 minutes to load the names of all the newsgroups onto your computer, but after that they open up in seconds whenever you want them.

nick – Nickname, – an alias you can give yourself and use when entering a chat channel, rather than using your real name.

Nominet – An official body for registering domain names in the UK (for exam-ple web sites whose name ends in .co.uk).

online – The time you spend linked via a modem to the internet. You can keep your phone bill down by reducing online time. The opposite term is offline.

open source software – A type of freely modifiable software, such as Linux. A definition and more information can be found at: www.opensource.org

OS – The operating system in a computer, for example MS DOS (Microsoft Disk Operating System), or Windows 95/98.

packet – The term for any small piece of data sent or received over the internet on your behalf by your internet service provider, and containing your address and the recipient's address. One email message for example may be trans-mitted as several different packets of information, and reassembled at the other end to recreate the message.

password – A word or series of letters and numbers that enables a user to access a file, computer or program. A passphrase is a password made by using more than one word.

PC – Personal computer.

Pentium – The name of a very popular microprocessor chip in personal com-puters, manufactured by Intel. The first Pentium IIIs were supplied with se-cret and unique personal identifiers, which ordinary people surfing the net were unwittingly sending out, enabling persons unknown to construct de-tailed user profiles. After a storm of protest, Pentium changed the technol-ogy so that this identifier could be disabled. If you buy or use a Pentium III computer you should be aware of this risk to your privacy when online.

Glossary of internet terms ....

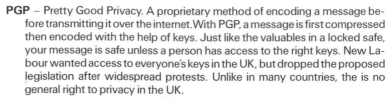

PGP Security Products

▶ Overview
  Gauntlet Firewall
  CyberCop
  PGP VPN
  PGP Data Security
  PGP E-Business
  Server
  PGP Developer Kit
  PGP Freeware
  WebShield

PGP – Pretty Good Privacy. A proprietary method of encoding a message before transmitting it over the internet. With PGP, a message is first compressed then encoded with the help of keys. Just like the valuables in a locked safe, your message is safe unless a person has access to the right keys. New Labour wanted access to everyone's keys in the UK, but dropped the proposed legislation after widespread protests. Unlike in many countries, the is no general right to privacy in the UK.

ping – You can use a ping test to check the connection speed between your computer and another computer.

plug-in – A type of (usually free and downloadable) software required to add some form of functionality to web page viewing. A well-known example is Macromedia Shockwave, a plug-in which enables you to view animations.

PoP – Point of presence. This refers to the dial-up phone numbers available from your ISP. If your ISP does not have a local point of presence (i.e. local access phone number), then don't sign up – your telephone bill will rocket because you will be charged national phone rates. All the major ISPs have local numbers covering the whole of the country.

portal site – Portal means gateway. It is a web site designed to be used as a starting point for your web experience each time you go online. Portals often serve as general information points and offer news, weather and other information that you can customise to your own needs. Yahoo! is a good example of a portal (http://www.yahoo.com). A portal site includes the one that loads into your browser each time you connect to the internet. It could for example be the front page of your internet service provider. Or you can set your browser to make it some other front page, for example a search engine such as AltaVista, or even your own home page if you have one.

post, to – The common term used for sending ('posting') messages to a newsgroup. Posting messages is very like sending emails, except of course that they are public and everyone can read them. Also, newsgroup postings are archived, and can be read by anyone in the world years later. Because of this, many people feel more comfortable using an 'alias' (made-up name) when posting messages.

privacy – You have practically no personal privacy online. Almost every mouse click and key stroke you make while online could be electronically logged, analysed and possibly archived by internet organisations, government agencies, police and other surveillance services. You are also leaving a permanent trail of data on whichever computer you are using. But then, if you have nothing to hide you have nothing to fear... To explore privacy issues worldwide visit the authoritative Electronic Frontier Foundation web site at www.eff.org and, for the UK, www.netfreedom.org

protocol – Technical term for the method by which computers communicate. A protocol is an agreed set of technical rules that can be used between systems. For example, for viewing web pages your computer would use hypertext transfer protocol (http). For downloading and uploading files, it would use file transfer protocol (ftp). It's not something to worry about in ordinary life.

proxy – An intermediate computer or server, used for reasons of security.

Quicktime – A popular free software program from Apple Computers. It is designed to play sounds and images including video clips and animations on both Apple Macs and personal computers.

refresh, reload – The refresh or reload button on your browser toolbar tells the web page you are looking at to reload.

register – You may have to give your name, personal details and financial information to some sites before you can continue to use the pages. Site owners may want to produce a mailing list to offer you products and services. Registration is also used to discourage casual traffic which can clog up access.

QuickTime™

registered user – Someone who has filled out an online form and then been granted permission to access a restricted area of a web site. Access is usually obtained by logging on, typically by entering a password and user name.

remailer – A remailer preserves your privacy by acting as a go-between when you browse or send email messages. An anonymous remailer is simply a computer connected to the internet that can forward an email message to other people after stripping off the header of the messages. Once a message is routed through an anonymous remailer, the recipient of that message, or anyone intercepting it, can no longer identify its origin.

RFC – Request for comment. RFCs are used by internet developers to propose changes and discuss standards and procedures. See http://rs.internic.net

RSA – A popular method of encryption, used in Netscape browsers. See http://www.rsa.com and see also PGP above.

router – A machine that directs – 'routes' – internet data (network packets) from one place to another.

rules – The term for message filters in Outlook Express.

search engine – A search engine is a web site you can use for finding something on the internet. Popular search engines are big web sites and information directories in their own right. There are hundreds of them; the best known include Alta Vista, Excite, Google, Infoseek, Lycos and Yahoo!.

secure servers – The hardware and software provided so that people can use their credit cards and leave other details without the risk of others seeing them online. Your browser will tell you when you are entering a secure site.

secure sockets layer (SSL) – A standard piece of technology which encrypts and secures financial transactions and data flow over the internet.

security certificate – Information used by the SSL protocol to establish a secure connection. Security certificates contain information about who it belongs to, who it was issued by, some form of unique identification, valid dates, and an encrypted fingerprint that can be used to verify the contents of the certificate. In order for an SSL connection to be created both sides must have a valid security certificate.

server – Any computer on a network that provides access and serves information to other computers.

shareware – Software that you can try before you buy. Usually there is some kind of limitation such as an expiry date. To get the registered version, you must pay for the software, typically $20 to $40. A vast amount of shareware is now available on the internet.

Shockwave – A popular piece of software produced by Macromedia, which enables you to view animations and other special effects on web sites. You can download it free and in a few minutes from Macromedia's web site. The effects can be fun, but they slow down the speed at which the pages load into your browser window.

signature file – This is a little text file in which you can place your address details, for adding to email and newsgroup messages. Once you have created a signature file, it is appended automatically to your emails. You can of delete or edit it.

Slashdot – One of the leading technology news web sites, found at: http://slashdot.org

smiley – A form of **emoticon.**

snail mail – The popular term for the standard postal service involving postpersons, vans, trains, planes, sacks and sorting offices.

spam – The popular term for electronic junk mail – unsolicited and unwelcome email messages sent across the internet. The term comes from Monty Python. There are various forms of spam-busting software which you can now obtain to filter out unwanted email messages.

sniffer – A program on a computer system (usually an ISP's system) designed to collect information about how people use the internet. Sniffers are often used by hackers to collect passwords and user names.

SSL – Secure socket layer, a key part of internet security technology.

subscribe – The term for accessing a newsgroup in order to read and post messages in the newsgroup. There is no charge, and you can subscribe, unsubscribe and resubscribe at will with a click of your mouse. Unless you post a message, no-one in the newsgroup will know that you have subscribed or unsubscribed.

surfing – Slang term for browsing the internet, especially following trails of links on pages across the world wide web.

sysop – Systems operator, someone rather like a moderator, for example, of a chat room or bulletin board service.

TCP/IP – Transmission control protocol/internet protocol, the essential technology of the internet. It's not normally something to worry about.

telnet – Software that allows you to connect via the internet to a remote computer and work as if you were a terminal linked to that system.

theme – A term in web page design. A theme describes the general colours and graphics used within a web site. Many themes are available in the form of ready-made templates.

thumbnail – A small version of a graphic file which, when clicked, expands to full size.

thread – An ongoing topic in a Usenet newsgroup or mailing list discussion. The term refers to the original message on a particular topic, and all the replies and other messages which spin off from it. With news reading software, you can easily 'view thread' and thus read the related messages in one convenient batch.

traceroute – A program that traces the route of a communication between your machine and a remote system. It is useful if you need to discover a person's ISP, for example in the case of a spammer.

traffic – The amount of data flowing across the internet to a particular web site, newsgroup or chat room, or as emails.

trojan horse – A program that seems to perform a useful task but is really a malevolent one designed to cause damage to a computer system.

uploading – The act of copying files from your PC to a server or other PC on the internet, for example when you are publishing your own web pages. The term is most commonly used to describe the act of copying HTML pages onto the internet via FTP.

UNIX – This is a computer operating system that has been in use for many years, and still is used in many larger systems. Most ISPs use it.

URL – Uniform resource locator – the address of each internet page, e.g. the URL of Internet Handbooks is http://www.internet-handbooks.co.uk

Usenet – The collection of well over 50,000 active newsgroups that make up a substantial part of the internet.

virtual reality – The presentation of a lifelike scenario in electronic form. It can be used for gaming, business or educational purposes.

virus – A computer program maliciously designed to cause havoc to people's computer files. Viruses can typically be received when downloading program files from the internet or copying material from infected disks. Even Word files can now be infected. You can protect yourself from the vast majority of them by installing some inexpensive anti-virus software, such as Norton, McAfee or Dr Solomon.

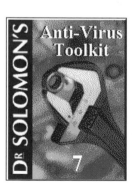

WAP – Wireless applications protocol, the technology that enables mobile phones to access the internet.

web authoring – Creating HTML pages to upload onto the internet. You will be a web author if you create your own home page for uploading onto the internet.

web client – Another term for a browser such as Internet Explorer or Netscape Navigator.

Webcrawler – A popular internet search engine used to find pages relating to specific keywords entered.

webmaster – Any person who manages a web site.

web page – Any single page of information you can view on the world wide web. A typical web page includes a unique URL (address), headings, text, images, and hyperlinks (usually in the form of graphic icons, or underlined text). One web page usually contains links to lots of other web pages, either within the same web site or elsewhere on the world wide web.

web rings – A network of interlinked web sites that share a common interest.

whois – A network service that allows you to consult a database containing information about someone. A whois query can, for example, help to find the identity of someone who is sending you unwanted email messages.

Windows – The ubiquitous operating system for personal computers developed by Bill Gates and the Microsoft Corporation. The Windows 3.1 version was followed by Windows 95, further enhanced by Windows 98. Windows 2000 is the latest.

WWW – The world wide web. Since it began in 1994 this has become the most popular part of the internet. The web is now made up of more than a billion web pages of every imaginable description, typically linking to other pages. Developed by the British computer scientist, Tim Berners-Lee, its growth has been exponential and is set to continue so.

WYSIWYG – 'What you see is what you get.' If you see it on the screen, then it should look just the same when you print it out.

Yahoo! – Probably the world's most popular internet directory and search engine, and now valued on Wall Street at billions of dollars: http://www.yahoo.com

zip/unzip – Many files that you download from the internet will be in compressed format, especially if they are large files. This is to make them quicker to download. These files are said to be zipped or compressed. Unzipping these compressed files means returning them to their original size on receipt. Zip files have the extension '.zip' and are created (and unzipped) using WinZip or a similar popular software package.

WAP.COM

OUR GUIDE TO THE WIRELESS INTERNET

TOOLS

- Pressroom
- WAP Glossary
- What is WAP?
- About us
- Feedback
- Free newsletter
- Register WAP link
- Win a WAP phone!
- Jobs@Wap.com
- Advertise?

Inside Yahoo!

- Yahoo! Address Book: Keep your contacts safe
- Web Access For Free! With Yahoo! Online
- New to Yahoo!? - For help click here

[more features...]

Visit the free Internet HelpZone at
www.internet-handbooks.co.uk
Helping you master the internet

Further reading

Activities for Using the Internet in Primary Schools, E Cico, M Farmer & C Hargrave (Kogan Page)

Adults Continuing Education Year Book (NIACE)

Building a Web Site on the Internet, Brendan Murphy (Internet Handbooks)

Careers Guidance on the Internet, Laurel Alexander (Internet Handbooks)

'Computer-Assisted and Open Access Education', R Land, *Aspects of Educational and Training Technology XXVII* (Kogan Page)

Creating a Home Page on the Internet, Richard Cochrane (Internet Handbooks)

Delivering Digitally, A Inglis, P Ling & V Joosten (Kogan Page)

'Developing and Measuring Competence', D Saunders P Race, *Aspects of Educational and Training Technology XXV* (Kogan Page)

Finding a Job on the Internet, David Holland (Internet Handbooks)

Finding a Job with a Future, Laurel Alexander (How To Books)

Getting Started on the Internet, Kye Valongo (Internet Handbooks)

'Implementing Flexible Learning', C Bell, M Bowden & A Trott, *Aspects of Educational and Training Technology XXIX* (Kogan Page)

Internet-Based Learning, D French, C Hale, C Johnson & G Farr (Kogan Page)

Internet for Schools, Barry Thomas & Richard Williams (Internet Handbooks)

Internet for Students, David Holland (Internet Handbooks)

Knowledge Web, M Eisenstadt & T Vincent (Kogan Page)

Learning New Job Skills, Laurel Alexander (How To Books)

Open and Flexible Learning in Vocational Education and Training, J Calder & A McCollum (Kogan Page)

Protecting Children on the Internet, Graham Jones (Internet Handbooks)

Studying English on the Internet, Wendy Shaw (Internet Handbooks)

Studying Law on the Internet, Stephen Hardy (Internet Handbooks)

Teaching and Learning Materials and the Internet, Ian Forsyth (Kogan Page)

Technology-Based Training, S Ravet & M Layte (Kogan Page)

Using the Internet in Secondary Schools, M Farmer, J Hargrave & E Cicco (Kogan Page)

Virtual University, H Freeman, T Routen, D Patel, S Ryan & B Scott (Kogan Page)

Where to Find It on the Internet, Kye Valongo (Internet Handbooks, 2nd edition)

Index

Index ....

Index ....